PRAY THROUGH IT

A Practical Guide to

Powerful and Effective Prayers

Shavaunta Harris

Printed in the United States of America in 2025.

ISBN: 979-8-21-867857-9
Library of Congress Control Number: 2025911706

Book and Cover Design
MaryG Publishing Consultants
www.marygpublishing.com
info@marygpublishing.com

For information about this book contact:
Shavaunta Harris
www.kcscribe.co
contact@kcscribe.co

Dedication

I want to dedicate this book to the man that loved me before my very first breath, and thought enough of me to love me knowing all my flaws and shortcomings. I dedicate this book to my Heavenly Father. He's my everything. I never knew just how you would use somebody like me. Thank you for waiting for me. I will forever live my life for your glory and forever lift up your name. This book would not be without you!

To my husband Dominique Harris. Your love, support, confidence and trust of the God in me is beyond words. Thank you for supporting and pushing me to be who God has called me to be! The love that you've shown is refreshing.

To my four beautiful children Jay, Cali, Genesis, and Dominique Jr. I thank God for giving me the privilege to be called your mother. Your existence keeps me in a place of prayer. I pray that you live a life of prayer, and never forget that your help is only one prayer away! I pray that my life will be an example of what a woman of prayer looks like. I love you!

To my mother Tabitha Dukes, one of the bravest women I know! You made the choice to give me life, and I am forever grateful for your love and sacrifice. Thank you for teaching me how to be strong, how to have values that were honorable and to live a life of integrity. I honor you; I value you; I appreciate you and love you!

Acknowledgements

To my sister in Christ Shelbra Woolridge for being the example of a woman of prayer. Thank you for praying with and for me when I could not pray for myself. You are an example of what it means to have praying friends. Thank you for challenging me, inspiring me, pushing me, encouraging me, correcting me and loving me, flaws and all. Words can't express just how thankful I am for you and your friendship! Love you Shel!

To Minister Gloria Terry, a woman who not only prayed for me but helped me see the call of intercession in me. I am thankful for the seeds of intercession you have continually sowed into my life over the years! I thank you for pushing forth and cultivating a heart for prayer. Thank you for continuing to live a life fully devoted to prayer! I love and appreciate you!

To Pastor Patrice Smith, thank you for your love, mentorship, encouragement and the gentle push that helped me grow. I thank God for allowing you to see greatness inside of me. You helped me build up confidence in the place of prayer. I will never forget the first time you put a mic in my hand and told me to pray. It was at that moment that I realized that there was something that the Lord placed in me that many would be blessed by. Thank you for everything.

I would also like to extend my heartfelt gratitude to the incredible contributors whose wisdom, testimonies, and insights have enriched this book:

- Amelia Mosley, for your inspiring story of faith and God's provision in times of need.
- Melissa Blacken, for revealing the intimacy we can have with God as our Heavenly Father.
- Apostle Brian Lewis Sr., for teaching on the power of faith and prayer amidst doubt and condemnation.
- Pastor Lesley Bradley, for highlighting fasting as a vital tool for spiritual focus and breakthrough.
- Minister Gloria Terry, for shedding light on the divine partnership established through prayer.
- Minister Shelbra Woolridge, for addressing the many barriers encountered in cultivating a prayer life.

Your contributions have brought depth and clarity, and I am truly thankful for your willingness to share your heart. May your words inspire and bless every reader as much as they have blessed me.

I'm grateful to every leader, past and present, who has prayed for me and poured into my life over the years—thank you. To those who planted seeds and those who faithfully watered them—thank you from the depths of my heart. I acknowledge every friend, sister and brother in Christ, and every word of encouragement given.

Contents

Chapter Seven: Prayers And Declarations

Introduction

Welcome to your personal journey of discovery into the heart of prayer! In this book, we are going to explore why prayer is so incredibly vital for believers like you and me. My goal is to arm you with the tools you need to enhance your prayer life—the most powerful weapon in your spiritual arsenal!

Let us start by understanding the sheer power packed into prayer. Did you know that God wants us to pray all the time? Yep, it is true! He desires constant communication with us, no matter what situation we find ourselves in (1 Thessalonians 5:16-17). It is His will that we are in touch with Him, always. You may be asking yourself, "Does God truly expect us to pray constantly?" The answer to that question is both yes and no. You might wonder, "How can I possibly maintain a constant state of prayer when I have so many responsibilities and tasks to attend to?"

When the Bible says, "pray always," it means to maintain a continual attitude of prayer throughout all aspects of life. It does not necessarily mean praying every single moment of the day without ceasing, but rather having a mindset of dependence on and communication with God in all circumstances at all times and to never cease doing so.

This includes regular times of focused prayer, as well as maintaining an ongoing conversation with God, seeking His guidance, and expressing gratitude throughout the day. The idea is to cultivate a lifestyle of prayer, integrating it into every aspect of your daily life.

Many believers overlook the incredible potential of prayer. We have been granted access to the heavenly courtroom, yet many of us miss out on its abundant benefits. If only we realized the authority and power that lies dormant within us, waiting to be unleashed through prayer! Through Jesus, God has given us great authority and power when we pray, both here on earth and in heaven. And guess what opens the door to accessing this power? You got it—prayer! Through prayer, we tap into incredible resources and promises that God has made available to us in His Word.

Take a closer look at a powerful passage in Matthew 18:18-20:

"I tell you the truth, whatever you forbid on earth will be forbidden in heaven, and whatever you permit on earth will be permitted in heaven. "I also tell you this: If two of you agree here on earth concerning anything you ask, my Father in heaven will do it for you. "For where two or three gather together as my followers, I am there among them."

This verse reveals a spiritual law of the kingdom of God that is powerful and very real—a system of authority operating beyond what our eyes can see. Just like there is a structured court system here on earth, there is a similar order in the Heavenly Realm. When we pray, we are essentially presenting our case before this heavenly court. Jesus gives us access to God and in the courts of heaven (Romans 8:34). He becomes our advocate and intercedes on our behalf. (1 John 2:1) And here is the amazing part—God is not only willing but eager to respond to our petitions. That's incredible right? Prayer is not limited to the walls of a church building or your prayer closet. Nope! Wherever two or three believers gather in Jesus' name, He is right there with them. So, whether you are praying alone or with others, know that God is listening, ready to answer, and eager to respond.

This is why I believe this book is essential. My hope is that by the end of this book, the veil of prayerlessness will be lifted from your eyes, you awaken to the truth of what Jesus accomplished on the cross and you pray with the power we have been given in prayer. Throughout these pages, we will delve into why prayer is absolutely essential for overcoming life's challenges through heavenly intervention. You will discover practical, transformative tools to aid you in your journey of growth in prayer, you will gain understanding of what hinders your prayers, learn some strategies how to overcome those hindrances, and build a strong foundation to growing in relationship with God through prayer.

This book will help guide you into a life of consistent, result-filled prayer, regardless of how tough or impossible the situations may seem. So, let us embark on this journey together with confidence and expectation. We will approach God with boldness, knowing that He is eagerly waiting to hear from us, and He will respond to our prayers. Together, we will unlock the extraordinary power of prayer and watch as God moves mightily in our lives. Get ready for an incredible journey! And remember, No matter the situation, God has given you the power and ability to PRAY THROUGH IT!

My Prayer For You

Father, I pray for your son or daughter who is reading this book right now. Some of them have never prayed before. Many of them have been praying and have not seen what they have been asking for. Some people need a fresh relationship with you, and some are close to giving up. Father, just as you strengthened Jesus in the garden of Gethsemane when He was getting ready to complete His assignment and journeying to the cross. We, your sons and daughters, are asking that you give us that same strength.

Lord as we take this journey together with you into a new place of prayer, as we accept this invitation to prayer, we ask that you set our prayer life a blaze. That the fire of prayer would burn within us. I am expecting you to give them strength for the journey. In times when it is hard, remind them to pray, in moments of struggle remind them to pray, when sadness, loss, hurt and pain show up in their homes like an uninvited guest; remind them to pray! As seasons change and people walk out of their lives, remind them to pray. I bind every hindrance that may get in the way of you speaking to them as they read this book and learn more about praying. I pray that there comes a seek and hunger for more intimacy with you in the place of prayer. I thank you that nothing can stand in the way of the intimate time that you are drawing them into. Father, release focus, confirmation, understanding, peace and the spirit of Jesus Christ Himself upon them to seek the

Father in all things through prayer and supplication! Jesus made it to the cross because through it all He remembered to pray!

Father, I ask you all of these things in faith and we put our faith into action. We believe in you for it, we have faith, and we are ready to grow in prayer. We will keep on asking, seeking and knocking. God, thank you for the invitation to deeper fellowship though prayer. It is in your son Jesus name we pray, Amen.

CHAPTER ONE

UNDERSTANDING PRAYER

What Prayer Is Not

P rayer is not a mere ritual, or empty words recited without sincerity. It is not a tool to manipulate God or to demand His compliance with our desires. True prayer is not about impressing others or highlighting one's spirituality. Prayer is not a final effort to get what we want from God. Prayer is not a way to manipulate and control others around us to do what we want. It is not about appearing to be religious or more spiritual than others. Let us take a look at biblical examples of what prayer is not.

1. **Empty Rituals:**

   "When you pray, don't babble on and on as the Gentiles do. They think their prayers are answered merely by repeating their words again and again." *(Matthew 6:7, NLT)*

2. **Self-centered Demands:**

   "And even when you ask, you don't get it because your motives are all wrong—you want only what will give you pleasure." *(James 4:3, NLT)*

3. Arrogant or Proud:

"The Pharisee stood by himself and prayed this prayer: 'I thank you, God, that I am not like other people—cheaters, sinners, adulterers. I am certainly not like that tax collector! I fast twice a week, and I give you a tenth of my income!'"
(Luke 18:11-12, NLT)

4. Without Faith:

"But when you ask him, be sure that your faith is in God alone. Do not waver, for a person with divided loyalty is as unsettled as a wave of the sea that is blown and tossed by the wind."
(James 1:6-7, NLT)

5. Hypocritical:

"When you pray, don't be like the hypocrites who love to pray publicly on street corners and in the synagogues where everyone can see them. I tell you the truth, that is all the reward they will ever get." *(Matthew 6:5, NLT)*

6. Disrespectful:

"Don't make rash promises, and don't be hasty in bringing matters before God. After all, God is in heaven, and you are here on earth. So let your words be few." *(Ecclesiastes 5:2, NLT)*

7. Doubtful:

"But when you ask him, be sure that your faith is in God alone. Do not waver, for a person with divided loyalty is as unsettled as a wave of the sea that is blown and tossed by the wind."

(James 1:6, NLT)

Prayer isn't something we do to check off our list. It should come before we begin our checklist. It isn't something that should be mundane or an afterthought. We should pray with expectation and excitement. Prayer isn't something we do when we are in trouble, it is a confident call to God for all our needs.

These examples highlight the importance of sincerity, humility, and faithfulness in prayer, as well as the need to align our hearts with God's will and character. God desires an authentic expression of our innermost thoughts and feelings before Him. Prayer is saying to God your advice is the advice that I treasure and value more than anything else. Payer reveals our heart for God to God.

"And when you pray, do not keep on babbling like pagans, for they think they will be heard because of their many words. Do not be like them, for your Father knows what you need before you ask him."

(Matthew 6:7-8, NIV)

The word *prayer* finds its origin in Greek, where the term is *Proseuchomai* (pros-yoo'-khom-ahe). Biblically, prayer entails supplication or direct interaction with God. It serves as a means of engaging with the Divine, fostering relationship, and communication with our Creator (Matthew 6:5-7). Just as we invest time and effort into nurturing relationships with those we love, prayer serves as the cornerstone for building a meaningful connection with God.

Your relationship with God should be the basis for all other relationships in your life. Any bond not grounded in your relationship with God risks fragility and failure. Prayer is the avenue through which we demonstrate our trust in God's wisdom and sovereignty. It acknowledges His control over our lives and prioritizes His guidance more than anything else. A believer who surrenders to God's will finds expression through prayer, offering God unrestricted access to their heart and life.

Through years of serving God, I have come to understand that prayer is not optional for believers; it is as essential as water is for sustaining life. Prayer rejuvenates our spirits, satiates our hunger for righteousness, and continues to position us to walk in victory. Even in the face of challenges, prayer instills confidence that victory is assured, regardless of appearances. Ephesians 6:12 reminds us that our struggles extend beyond the physical realm, encompassing spiritual battles against unseen forces of darkness. In spiritual warfare, prayer becomes our most powerful weapon against our invisible enemy, empowering us to overcome adversities. While our struggles manifest in the natural world, their roots lie in the spiritual realm.

The resources needed to confront these challenges are in the Bible, and victory is attained through understanding and leveraging the power of prayer. Therefore, let us embrace prayer as a vital lifeline connecting us to God's strength and provision. In prayer, we tap into God's unlimited power and find the courage to face every trial with confidence, knowing that He who is in us is greater than any challenge we may encounter (1 John 4:4).

What Is Prayer?

The simplest definition of prayer is the sacred communication between people and God. It is the way through which we express our gratitude, seek guidance, find peace, and deepen our relationship with the Divine Creator. In prayer, we open our hearts and minds to God's presence, acknowledging His sovereignty and seeking His will. Though I have given you a simple definition, let us take a look at what the bible says prayer is. Here are some scriptural insights into what constitutes biblical prayer:

1. **Reverence**:
   "Come, let us worship and bow down. Let us kneel before the Lord our maker." *(Psalm 95:6, NLT)*

2. **Faith:**

"You can pray for anything, and if you have faith, you will receive it." *(Matthew 21:22 , NLT)*

3. **Humility:**

"Humble yourselves before the Lord, and he will lift you up in honor." *(James 4:10, NLT)*

4. **Alignment with God's Will**:

"And we are confident that he hears us whenever we ask for anything that pleases him." *(1 John 5:14, NLT)*

5. **Persistence:**

"One day Jesus told his disciples a story to show that they should always pray and never give up." *(Luke 18:1, NLT)*

6. **Thanksgiving:**

"Don't worry about anything; instead, pray about everything. Tell God what you need, and thank him for all he has done." *(Philippians 4:6, NLT)*

7. **Confession:**

"But if we confess our sins to him, he is faithful and just to forgive us our sins and to cleanse us from all wickedness." *(1 John 1:9, NLT)*

Biblical prayer involves pouring out our hearts to God, seeking His guidance, acknowledging His sovereignty, and aligning our desires with His will. It is both a privilege and a responsibility for believers to communicate with God through prayer.

Biblical Examples Of Prayer

Throughout the Bible, we find numerous examples of individuals engaging in prayer, demonstrating its significance and power in their lives.

1. **The Lord's Prayer** - Matthew 6:9-13, Jesus teaches His disciples the model prayer, known as the Lord's Prayer. It serves as a blueprint for addressing God with reverence, seeking His kingdom, and surrendering to His will.

2. **Hannah's Prayer** - 1 Samuel 1:10-20, Hannah pours out her heart to God, seeking a child. Her fervent prayer is answered, and she gives birth to Samuel, who becomes a great prophet in Israel.

3. **Daniel's Prayer** - Daniel 9:3-19 illustrates repentance, humility, and intercession on behalf of his people. Despite facing opposition, Daniel remains steadfast in prayer, demonstrating unwavering faith in God's promises.

4. **Jesus' Prayer in Gethsemane** - Matthew 26:36-46, Jesus models profound submission to the Father's will in prayer. He prays earnestly before His crucifixion, demonstrating trust in God's plan despite the agony He anticipates.

These biblical examples highlight the diversity of prayers offered to God, ranging from petitions, to praise, from intercession to thanksgiving. They inspire us to approach God with honesty, faith, and humility in our own prayer lives. As we delve deeper into the practice of prayer, may we draw closer to God, experiencing His presence and power in our daily lives. Let us emulate the faith of those who have gone before us, trusting in God's faithfulness as we lift our hearts to Him in prayer.

God has taken away any excuse we could have for not praying. When it is hard to pray, pray anyway. When we do not know what to say, Romans 8:26 says the Holy Spirit will pray for us with groanings that cannot be expressed through words.

Who Is Called To Pray?

When we think about prayer, it's often associated with a select few—the seasoned church leaders, intercessors, or that one family member who seems to have a "direct line" to God. Like many, I believed prayer was reserved for people who "had it together" spiritually—those who could speak eloquently or move a room with passionate petitions to God. I would sit back, and watch others pray, wondering how their words carried so much power. Their prayers felt like thunder in the heavens, while mine felt like whispers lost in the wind. Have you ever felt like your words were not enough?

Let me tell you something: God is not moved by fancy words or long speeches. He is moved by your heart. He does not measure prayers by eloquence or experience, but by sincerity and faith. Remember Hannah in 1 Samuel 1? She prayed in such anguish and desperation for a child that Eli, the priest, thought she was drunk! Yet God heard her heart. Hannah didn't pray with polished words or a prepared script; she prayed with a raw and honest heart, and God answered her.

The truth is prayer is not for a select group of people; it is for everyone. Yes, you are called to pray, too. Jesus emphasized this when He taught His disciples how to pray in Matthew 6:9-13.

He did not tell them to wait until they were spiritual giants or seasoned believers; He simply said, "When you pray..." not "if" you pray. Jesus expects all of us to pray because it is our connection to the Father.

Let us take a moment to talk about Jesus. He was fully God and fully man, yet He still prayed. That speaks volumes! In Mark 1:35, we see Him rising early in the morning to spend time with the Father. Before He chose the twelve disciples, He spent the whole night in prayer (Luke 6:12). Even in the Garden of Gethsemane, the night He was betrayed, He prayed fervently (Luke 22:39–46). If Jesus, the Son of God, needed prayer to fulfill His purpose, how much more do we?

When I first felt that pull toward prayer, I did not know what to do with it. It was like an invisible hand drawing me closer, but I still wrestled with feelings of inadequacy. I did not realize at the time that it was the Holy Spirit inviting me into deeper intimacy with God.
Romans 8:26 tells us that the Spirit helps us in our weakness and intercedes on our behalf with groanings too deep for words. So even when you do not know what to say, the Holy Spirit steps in to help you communicate with God.

It was not until I joined my church's prayer team that I started to understand what prayer was really about. I realized that prayer was not a chore or a performance—it was a relationship. It was about talking to my Heavenly Father, pouring out my heart, and learning to hear His voice. There is nothing more powerful than hearing God's voice for yourself.

But what does it mean to hear God's voice? It does not always come as a loud, audible sound. Sometimes it is a whisper in your spirit, a verse that comes alive, or a peace that surpasses understanding. Just like Elijah experienced in 1 Kings 19, God often speaks in a "still small voice." And to hear it, we must quiet ourselves in prayer and be attentive to His presence.

Now, let me tell you something else: prayer is not just about changing circumstances; it is about changing you. Think about the story of Peter in Acts 12. He was in prison, chained between two guards, but the church was praying fervently for him. God responded by sending an angel to free Peter from his chains. That is the power of prayer! It moves mountains, breaks chains, and brings about supernatural breakthroughs. But even more than that, prayer transforms our hearts, aligns us with God's will, and strengthens our faith.

You might wonder, "Why does God want me to pray if He already knows everything?" The answer is simple: God wants a relationship with you. He doesn't just want to be your problem-solver or your 911 call in emergencies. He wants to walk with you daily, to hear your joys, your struggles, your fears, and your dreams. Just like a loving parent wants to hear their child's voice, God wants to hear yours.

Scripture is clear that God desires for everyone to pray. Luke 18:1 says, "men ought always to pray and not faint." 1 Thessalonians 5:17 reminds us to "pray without ceasing." And in Jeremiah 33:3, God gives us this promise: "Call to me and I will answer you and tell you great and unsearchable things you do not know." God is waiting for us to call on Him. He's not distant or unreachable; He's right here, ready to listen and respond.

So, let me ask you: Are you ready to start praying, no matter where you are in your walk with God? It doesn't matter if you have been saved for years or if you are just getting to know Him. God is not waiting for perfection; He is waiting for your surrender.

As Philippians 4:6–7 reminds us:

"Do not be anxious about anything, but in every situation, by prayer and petition, with thanksgiving, present your requests to God. And the peace of God, which transcends all understanding, will guard your hearts and your minds in Christ Jesus."

I pray that as you read this, the fire of prayer ignites in your heart. I pray that you experience God in a way that makes you hunger for more of Him, that prayer becomes your lifeline, your refuge, and your source of strength. Remember, your help is just one prayer away. So do not hesitate. Start praying today—and do not stop!

CHAPTER TWO

WHY DO WE NEED TO PRAY?

Does prayer feel like a chore to you? Is your prayer life non-existent? Are you struggling to maintain consistency in the place of prayer? Have you been called to pray but do not know where to begin? Have you ever felt hesitant to ask an obvious question about prayer? Have you found yourself wanting to pray but unsure how to start? Does prayer seem like a duty, something you only engage in when you are in trouble or need help? If you resonate with any of these questions, know that you are not alone.

I remember a time when I had related questions and concerns cluttering my mind and weighing me down. These uncertainties often deterred and frustrated me in my prayer life. If you have experienced any of these struggles, you are familiar with the feelings of praying without answers, battling doubts, and even ceasing to pray altogether.

Let me reassure you: being in such a place is not necessarily bad. While God desires us to pray and commands us to pray about everything all the time (1 Thessalonians 5:16-18), He can meet us wherever we are in our prayer journey. Your honesty with yourself and God about your prayer life is key to experiencing its power and consistency.

So, if you're feeling overwhelmed by some of these same struggles, have some of these questions or are struggling with prayer, know that you should expect and will be met with opposition when it comes to praying (read Daniel 10:12-13 and Ephesians 6:12 as they give an example of how we can be opposed and what opposes us in our prayer lives). Many believers have grappled with similar uncertainties at some point in their journey. This is the reality for many Christian believers today who have yet to discover the beauty and power of prayer. However, I have faith that God will reveal the power and authority that is in prayer as you journey through my book.

Praying has many purposes in our lives. God desires us to always pray for several reasons:

- **Relationship**: Prayer fosters intimacy and relationship with God. Just as communication is vital in any relationship, prayer is how we communicate with God, sharing our thoughts, feelings, and concerns while also listening to Him.

- **Dependence:** Through prayer, we acknowledge our dependence on God. It is an admission that we cannot navigate life's challenges on our own and need His guidance, wisdom, and strength.

- **Alignment:** Prayer helps align our will with God's will. When we pray, "Your kingdom come, Your will be done," we surrender our desires to God's perfect plan for our lives.

- **Spiritual Warfare:** Prayer is a weapon in spiritual warfare. It enables us to stand firm against the enemy's schemes, to resist temptation, and to overcome trials and obstacles.

- **Transformation:** Prayer is transformative. It changes us from the inside out, conforming us to the image of Christ. As we spend time in God's presence, our character, attitudes, and perspectives are molded according to His purposes.

As we pray with a deep longing for God's presence, we grow to recognize just how much we depend on Him to change our desires for His. When we approach our Heavenly Father in prayer, we invite the supernatural into the natural realm. In moments of challenge and fierce opposition, we have the Helper (The Holy Spirit) whom we can call upon to intercede on our behalf or provide guidance on overcoming our adversaries.

Throughout scripture, prayer is consistently intertwined with God's divine intervention. God has removed every excuse we might have for neglecting prayer.

Even when it feels difficult to pray, we must press on. And in times of uncertainty, Romans 8:26 assures us that the Holy Spirit intercedes for us with groanings too deep for words.

When you take on the assignment to pray, you are also saying yes to God, not only to pray for your needs but for the needs of others. Your lifestyle of prayer is not selfish but selfless. As you accept the invitation to pray to the Father, He will begin to place the burdens of your family, friends, church, community, neighborhood, nation, country, and the world on your heart to pray and to do so without ceasing.

This is what we call intercession. A deep hunger and love will begin to grow between you and the Father. You are a believer, and called to pray for one another. There will be burdens that only you feel and sense, and it is your responsibility to take that burden seriously and respond to the invitation of the Lord to partner with Him in prayer.

You should never feel alone in your prayer life, but even if you do, you have to know that you are not because the Father is with you. God has not called you to be in prayer independent of Him but completely dependent upon Him. You cannot maintain your prayer life without strength and complete dependence on God. In your Christian walk, you were never called to do anything apart from God (John 15:5), and that includes prayer.

Facts About Prayer

Allow me to share several truths about prayer. As I am currently writing this book, I cannot help but notice a prevailing theme in the church right now that suggests prayer is not as powerful or as necessary as it once was. There is a generation that believes they can function as their own gods, bypassing the need for divine guidance. Instead of seeking God for answers, they rely on their own understanding and then attach God's name to their actions. This disregard for seeking God's guidance reflects a concerning trend. In this era, it is crucial to grasp the truth of God's Word regarding our daily living, principles, and prayer.

Let us explore these truths about prayer:

- **Prayer is your right as a believer.**
  "Because of Christ and our faith in him, we can now come boldly and confidently into God's presence." *(Ephesians 3:12)*

- **Prayer is necessary and needed.**
  "Never stop praying." *(1 Thessalonians 5:17)*

- **Prayers draw us close so that we can know the Father's heart.**
  "Come close to God, and God will come close to you." *(James 4:8)*

- **Prayer releases angelic hosts and divine intervention.**

  "For he will order his angels to protect you wherever you go. They will hold you up with their hands so you won't even hurt your foot on a stone." *(Psalm 91:11-12)*

- **Prayer invites God's kingdom into the earth.**

  "Your kingdom come, your will be done, on earth as it is in heaven." *(Matthew 6:10)*

- **Prayer provokes a response from God.**

  "Ask me and I will tell you remarkable secrets you do not know about things to come." *(Jeremiah 33:3)*

- **Prayer is a weapon!**

  "We use God's mighty weapons, not worldly weapons, to knock down the strongholds of human reasoning and to destroy false arguments." *(2 Corinthians 10:4)*

- **Prayer delights God's ear and melts His heart.**

  "O Lord, hear my plea for justice. Listen to my cry for help. Pay attention to my prayer, for it comes from honest lips." *(Psalm 17:1)*

- **Prayer helps you to resist temptation.**

  "And don't let us yield to temptation, but rescue us from the evil one." *(Matthew 6:13)*

- **Prayer must be the companion of every believer.**

  "Rejoice in our confident hope. Be patient in trouble, and keep on praying." *(Romans 12:12)*

- **Prayer is the key to heaven and faith opens the door.**

  "You can pray for anything, and if you have faith, you will receive it." *(Matthew 21:22)*

No matter your role—pastor, intercessor, teacher, prophet, apostle, evangelist, brother, or sister in the Lord—remember this: never let life's circumstances hinder your prayer life. Prayer is vital to us! The enemy understands this truth, and the gravest mistake we can make is neglecting what God has revealed in His Word about prayer, thereby missing witnessing His power in our lives. As we conclude this section, I want to leave you with three scriptures to encourage you:

1. "Let us hold tightly without wavering to the hope we affirm, for God can be trusted to keep his promise." *(Hebrews 10:23)*
2. "Rejoice in our confident hope. Be patient in trouble, and keep on praying." *(Romans 12:12)*

3. "In those days when you pray, I will listen."
   (Jeremiah 29:12, NLT)

My friend's trouble will come, know that, expect that, but always remember your help is only one prayer away.

"You can do more than pray after you have prayed, but you cannot do more than pray until you have prayed."
~ S.D. Gordon, Quiet Talks on Prayer

Benefits available to believers through Jesus when we pray

Through God's divine power, He has equipped us with everything necessary to live a life that reflects His character (2 Peter 1:3). As followers of Christ, we are recipients of many benefits as we walk with Him. He generously provides us with every spiritual gift needed to honor and glorify Him. While this list is not exhaustive and is not presented in any particular order, here are seven key benefits available to every believer who prays in alignment with God's will.

1. **Access to the Father:** Through Jesus' sacrifice, we have direct access to the Father in prayer. "For through him we both have access to the Father by one Spirit." *(Ephesians 2:18)*

2. **Confidence and Boldness:** We can approach God with confidence and boldness in prayer because of Jesus' sacrifice. "Let us then approach God's throne of grace with confidence, so that we may receive mercy and find grace to help us in our time of need." *(Hebrews 4:16)*

3. **Forgiveness of Sins:** Through prayer, we can seek and receive forgiveness of sins because of Jesus' atonement. "If we confess our sins, he is faithful and just and will forgive us our sins and purify us from all unrighteousness." *(1 John 1:9)*

4. **Intercession of the Holy Spirit:** The Holy Spirit intercedes for us in prayer, helping us pray according to God's will. "In the same way, the Spirit helps us in our weakness. We do not know what we ought to pray for, but the Spirit himself intercedes for us through wordless groans." *(Romans 8:26)*

5. **Assurance of Answered Prayer:** We have assurance that God hears and answers our prayers when we pray according to His will. "This is the confidence we have in approaching God: that if we ask anything according to his will, he hears us." *(1 John 5:14)*

6. **Empowerment for Miracles:** Through prayer, we can see miracles and mighty works accomplished in Jesus' name. "Therefore I tell you, whatever you ask for in prayer, believe that you have received it, and it will be yours." *(Mark 11:24)*

7. **Fellowship with God:** Prayer enables us to commune with God, deepening our relationship with Him. "We proclaim to you what we ourselves have actually seen and heard so that you may have fellowship with us. And our fellowship is with the Father and with his Son, Jesus Christ." *(1 John 1:3, NLT)*

We can also see the benefits of prayer through these men and women in the bible. These are just a few examples of the benefits available to believers when we put our faith in praying in Jesus name.

Your prayers have the power to heal:

- Prayer was the tool to which Abraham used to heal Abimelech and his family in Genesis. "Then Abraham prayed to God, and God healed Abimelech, his wife, and his female servants, so they could have children." *(Genesis 20:17)*

Your prayers are heard through pain:

- Hannah prayed to the lord in her anguish and through tears. "Hannah was in deep anguish, crying bitterly as she prayed to the LORD." *(1 Samuel 1:10)*

I want to challenge your thinking about prayer. My desire is that, regardless of the conditions, through prayer you will have the ability to outlast the fiery trials of life. Prayer can leave its mark on generations before and after your existence. Your very existence right now is the result of someone praying for you (Jesus praying for all believers in John 17). Prayers have the ability to produce tangible results from an invisible place. There is a prayer shift that occurs, which you can tangibly see take place in your life.

You might have heard people say, "What difference would it make for me to keep praying? I have been praying and nothing has happened." However, there is no comparison to the power accessed through prayer. Prayer is the vehicle to which the Holy Spirit drives, to bring us our answer from God. It is absolutely vital for our spiritual growth.

The Bible tells us that we should be constantly praying (1 Thessalonians 5:17) because prayer is the link between the spiritual and physical worlds. Connecting and accessing authority in the spiritual world can only happen through prayer.

God already knows what you want to talk about, but He wants to know if you want to talk to Him about it. We ask others to pray for us, and sometimes we hear them say, "It's already done!" However, there is a difference between something being available to us and having access to it. Through Jesus, God made every good thing available to us—prayer is how we access them and align our hearts with His will.

Think of it like being in a room with a glass wall between you and what you need. You can see everything you need on the other side but cannot access it. However, the moment you open your mouth in prayer, it forms a door that gives you access to what you see.

God desires an intimate, authentic relationship with us. He is not interested in a public display of affection without any private desire for a relationship. He wants our full, undivided attention. He wants a relationship with us that burns so deeply that it cannot be quenched by fiery trials and situations. This is why spending time praying is crucial. We must desire to be in God's presence like an awe-struck couple in love, wanting to spend time with Him intimately.

When we pray, we are saying to God, "You are important to me. I need you to lead me and guide me. Show me Your way, God."

In prayer, we seek God's instruction, wisdom, and plans for our lives. Just like Moses sought God's guidance and David sought God's counsel, we can unlock the secrets of God and know His plan for us through prayer and fellowship with Him intimately. Having the privilege of conversing with our Creator and nurturing a relationship with Him is truly remarkable. God eagerly anticipates hearing your voice in prayer because everything that concerns you matters to Him deeply. He longs for you to approach Him in prayer because He genuinely cares for you and desires intimate communion with you (see Jeremiah 29:12).

Moreover, prayer equips us to withstand the trials and challenges that life presents. Even as I write this book, I frequently pause to pray. The enemy often attempts to hinder our prayers, but it is imperative that we persevere. Prayer is not merely an option; it is a divine mandate. Our connection with God is established and strengthened through prayer. In prayer, we receive divine strength, revelation, answers, and assistance. Countless individuals have experienced healing and deliverance through prayer, and I can attest to its transformative power.

Prayer serves as our weapon and tool in navigating life's struggles. While praying does not guarantee an end to warfare, it empowers us to stand firm in the midst of battle, relying on the Lord's strength and might. As Ephesians 6:10 reminds us, we are to be strengthened by the Lord and to stand firm in His power.

Prayers for the generations to come:

- Our prayers serve as a testament for the generations that will follow after us. Just as the generation in the book of Kings cried out for the promised land despite never witnessing it themselves, our prayers echo through time, leaving behind a legacy for those who come after us. The prayers of our ancestors stand as monuments, reminding future generations that there is more to come, that there is power in the prayers of our foremothers and forefathers. Many of us can attest to the profound impact of prayer in our lives – prayers that spared us, shaped us, planned for us, and directed us.

- As we pray, we do so not just for ourselves but for the generations yet to come. Our prayers lay a foundation of faith, instilling in future generations the knowledge that prayer is potent and that our unchanging God remains steadfast throughout time.

Our prayer lives are part of a grander plan orchestrated by God for His people, a plan in which His glory is revealed, His kingdom established on earth, and His will made manifest.

- It is our duty to teach our children and grandchildren about the power of prayer, to show them how to commune with God who holds their futures in His hands. We must not neglect this responsibility, for by imparting the importance of prayer, we equip the next generation to stand on God's promises, to resist the darkness that surrounds them, and to fulfill the purpose God has ordained for them. Let us pray with intention, with focus, with the future in mind, so that the torch of prayer may be passed on from generation to generation, ensuring that God's kingdom continues to reign on earth.

- Ultimately, our role as men and women of God is to lead generations to come into a deep relationship with the Almighty through prayer. We must guide them to seek God's will more than anything else, to build a personal relationship with Him, and to live out the purpose He has ordained for them. Let us not be the generation that leads our descendants astray due to neglecting the vital practice of prayer. Instead, let us fervently pray for God's kingdom to come on earth as it is in heaven, securing a legacy of faithfulness and devotion to God for generations to come.

- Prayer grants us the ability to touch the intangible, to perceive the invisible realm. What once eluded our sight and grasp becomes tangible through prayer. We access the presence of our Father, who holds the world in His hands, and are empowered to speak forth His will into our lives.

- In times of uncertainty, prayer is our sole refuge. As I pen these words, our nation, and the world grapple with unprecedented challenges – closures of businesses, schools, and entire cities. The current lockdown leaves millions without work, urging us to isolate and distance ourselves. In such moments, the need for prayer becomes more evident.

- Traditionally, people seek solace within the walls of churches, but now, with doors closed and services suspended, we are compelled to seek God in unconventional places – on our knees in bathrooms, in our cars, or hidden away in closets. Amidst the panic and fear, prayer offers a sanctuary, a place of calm and assurance.

- Frequently, our prayers are focused on God changing circumstances or people around us. We plead for changes in our colleagues, spouses, or situations, unaware that persistent prayer can also bring about a transformation within ourselves. Prayer has the power to change us, but only if we allow it to do so.

- Consistent, fervent, and sincere prayer ensures that we, as children of God, do not emerge from battles empty-handed. Continuous prayer unleashes God's power to act in your life and defeat your enemies. "Your right hand, O LORD, glorious in power, your right hand, O LORD, shatters the enemy."
(Exodus 15:6). Battles fought in prayer are also won in prayer. When life becomes challenging, remember that prayer is the ultimate weapon to emerge victoriously. Prayer kindles an unquenchable fire within our souls, fostering unwavering assurance and trust in God, regardless of the circumstances.

My prayer for you is that you develop an insatiable appetite for prayer, feeling unable to move forward without seeking the Father. As you read this book, may God impart within you a steadfast allegiance to prayer and God's word, enabling you to persistently ask, seek, and knock, whether in isolation or facing giants.

"Prayer is indestructible! There is nothing on this earth that can stop prayer." – Shavaunta Harris

---

Prayerlessness

What is prayerlessness and how do we recognize it in our lives? What causes it and how do we combat it? Prayerlessness is a term that speaks to the lack of prayer or failure to pray. It describes a life or period where prayer is absent or minimal. Prayerlessness can manifest in many ways, such as forgetting to pray, not making time for prayer, or deliberately choosing not to engage in prayer. It signifies a disconnect from God and a failure to communicate with Him through prayer. Prayerlessness can hinder spiritual growth, weaken one's relationship with God, and lead to spiritual drifting, and a sense of spiritual dryness or distance.

Do you realize that your struggle with prayer is not just about discipline but also about faith? One of the simplest yet powerful demonstrations of the connection between prayer and faith is in Matthew 21:22. Let us explore this together.

- "You can pray for anything, and if you have faith, you will receive it." *(Matthew 21:22)*

Upon reading this, one might mistakenly assume that whatever we ask for, God will give it to us if we have faith. However, it is crucial to clarify that this is not what Jesus is implying. Instead, we need to consider the context carefully. Matthew 21:22 in context is part of a passage where Jesus is teaching his disciples and the crowds about faith and prayer. In the broader context, Jesus has just cursed a fig tree that had no fruit, and it withered immediately.

This event sparked a discussion with his disciples about the power of faith and prayer. Jesus is emphasizing that when we pray with genuine faith in God's ability to answer, nothing is impossible. However, this does not mean that we can pray for anything we want selfishly; rather, it draws to focus the importance of aligning our prayers with God's will and having trust in Him to fulfill His promises.

Matthew 21:22 teaches us about the significance of faith-filled prayer and the assurance that God responds to the prayers of those who trust in Him wholeheartedly. When we are saved and accept Jesus as our savior, we are armed with the weapon of prayer. Though we have this weapon many believers rarely use it. If we do not pray we will become prey. What we do not oppose we come into agreement with.

Oftentimes our warfare is so strong because we agree or have not opened up our mouths to challenge what is being said and done in the invisible realm. So as a result, what we see in the physical realm is a manifestation of what we have given authority to in the spiritual realm due to our lack of prayer. A prayerless believer is a powerless believer.

As a follower of Christ, God has called us to always pray. When we go without prayer, what we are saying is we know what is best for our lives. In other words, we are saying we are God, and He is not. Jesus is a notable example of what it means to pray and not cease. As we study Jesus' life we see that prayer was an integral part of His life and ministry.

The Gospels frequently mention Jesus praying at various points, such as before important decisions, during moments of solitude, and in times of distress. Jesus' emphasis of prayer in His life and ministry points us to the value that prayer should hold in our lives. Failure to pray or prioritize prayer in our day-to-day living can lead to issues like frustration, apathy, indifference toward God and drifting from Him. I want to touch on the topic of drifting as many believers are impacted by this and because it is so subtle we do not often recognize it.

Drifting

Drifting often stems from neglecting prayer. While its effects may not be immediately evident in the life of a believer, it is a subtle and gradual process, which makes drifting even more perilous. We should regularly assess the state of our prayer life. Let us delve deeper into the concept of drifting.

As someone who learns and thinks visually, I find it helpful to illustrate why prayerlessness poses a significant danger to believers. To provide a clearer explanation, let me paint a picture of what drifting looks like for a boat, and then draw a parallel between a boat's drift and how prayerlessness can cause us to drift. A boat drifts when it moves across the water without being under direct control or guidance. Several factors contribute to drifting. Let's take a look at what these factors are.

- **Wind:** Wind plays a pivotal role in boat drifting. It exerts force against the boat's sails or hull, propelling it in the direction of the wind's gusts. The intensity and direction of the wind can significantly influence the boat's drift. Just as boats are affected by the winds, our lives are often impacted by the unforeseen circumstances and challenges we face.

   "Then we will no longer be immature like children. We won't be tossed and blown about by every wind of new teaching. We will not be influenced when people try to trick us with lies so clever they sound like the truth." *(Ephesians 4:14)*

   Prayer is a testament to our trust in God. When life's storms and winds disrupt our peace and shake our stability, it serves as a reminder to turn to God in prayer. Many of the issues we encounter are beyond our control, catching us off guard and leaving us helpless to alter the outcome. However, in the face of adversity, prayer becomes our anchor, guiding us through turbulent waters and directing us toward God's wisdom, instruction, and direction. Thus, when the storms of life rage, let us not forget to seek God's face more fervently than ever before, knowing that He is our refuge and strength amidst our storms.

- **Currents:** Ocean currents, rivers, or tides exert a powerful influence on a boat's drift. These natural water movements can propel a boat even in the absence of wind. The direction and speed of currents vary, creating diverse drift patterns for boats navigating through them.

Before setting sail, sailors meticulously assess the current and wind conditions, recognizing the critical importance of this step for their safety. Similarly, we should approach our prayer life with the same level of urgency and vigilance. While we cannot foresee the daily challenges that may arise, we bear the responsibility of monitoring the conditions of our prayer life.

Rather than reacting to unexpected changes, we must proactively engage in prayer, remaining watchful for any dangers that may emerge. Scripture admonishes us in Matthew 26:41 to "Keep watch and pray, so that you will not give in to temptation. For the spirit is willing, but the body is weak." Despite the inclination of our flesh toward prayerlessness, the Spirit within us remains willing. Thus, by staying vigilant and prayerful, we can overcome any unforeseen currents that come our way.

- **Underpowered or Unpowered:** When a boat lacks sufficient power from its engine or sails, it struggles to resist the forces of wind or current, leading to drifting. Similarly, if the boat's engine fails or its sails are disabled, it can drift without control. An underpowered boat is one that cannot reach its destination. To be honest, I found myself in this place in my prayer life before. At times, I tried to pursue God's call based solely on yesterday's prayers, doing what I thought was best and relying on my own strength without seeking God's guidance. Sometimes, I acted out of my own flesh rather than the Spirit because I neglected to empower myself through prayer.

It often begins with skipping a day, then two, and before you know it, weeks have passed, and you have fallen into a pattern of daily drifting. You come to realize, much like the underpowered boat, you are aimlessly drifting. I know that feeling, and I can testify—it is not a good one.

Just like an underpowered boat struggle's against the forces of wind and currents, we too lack the power to resist the attacks of the enemy and the challenges of daily life without prayer. Ephesians 6:10 reminds us, "Finally, be strong in the Lord and in his mighty power."

I want to stress that it is His power that we need, not our own. Acting in our own strength often leads to aimless drifting. God has bestowed upon us the power to overcome. Our strength and ability come from the Lord, and we can only tap into it through prayer. I frequently remind myself and others that, "A prayerless person is a powerless person." Our capacity to stand firm against drifting from God can only be achieved by staying connected and empowered by Him through prayer and studying His word.

- **Inefficient Steering:** When the boat's operator fails to steer properly, drifting can occur. If the boat's rudder or steering mechanism is not correctly adjusted, or if the operator fails to account for wind and currents, the boat may drift off course. Navigating through the waters of life can be daunting, stressful, and overwhelming. Just as a boat needs a skilled sailor or captain, we too require guidance. Jesus promised us a Captain for our boat to help navigate through life and keep us on course—that Captain is the Holy Spirit.

    o Romans 8:26 (NLT) assures us, "And the Holy Spirit helps us in our weakness. For example, we do not know what God wants us to pray for. But the Holy Spirit prays for us with groanings that cannot be expressed in words."

    o John 14:16 (NLT) declares, "And I will ask the Father, and he will give you another Advocate, who will never leave you."

o   John 14:26 (NLT) states, "But when the Father sends the Advocate as my representative—that is, the Holy Spirit—he will teach you everything and will remind you of everything I have told you."

With the Holy Spirit as our Advocate, Comforter, and Helper, we need not fear our boat drifting off course, being lost, or not knowing which way to go. He steers us in God's direction, never leaving us alone. Even in moments when words fail us, we can rely on the Holy Spirit's guidance. As John 16:13 (NLT) says, "When the Spirit of truth comes, he will guide you into all truth." When words fail, and tears are all we have, God understands. So, call upon the Captain of your boat—He will hear and respond.

- **Anchoring Issues:** If a boat's anchor is not properly set or if the anchor line is too short or improperly secured, the boat may drift away from its intended position. "We have this hope as an anchor for the soul, firm and secure. *(Hebrews 6:19, NIV)* It enters the inner sanctuary behind the curtain."

This verse uses the metaphor of an anchor to describe the hope we have in God. Just as an anchor keeps a ship steady during storms and turbulent waters, our hope in God serves as a firm and secure anchor for our souls, providing stability and assurance, especially in challenging times.

Drifting can lead to significant problems for boats, including hazards like colliding with other vessels or becoming lost in dangerous waters. Boat operators must grasp the factors contributing to drifting and take prompt action to prevent or correct it. This may involve adjusting sails, using engines to counteract the drift, or securely anchoring the boat. Similarly, spiritual drifting often occurs subtly, creeping up on us without immediate notice.

Life-changing events such as job loss, illness, financial hardship, or personal trauma can gradually push us into a state of prayerlessness, especially when we are already struggling. However, the Scriptures repeatedly urge us to cry out to the Lord for help, assuring us of His response. No matter how challenging our circumstances, we must remember that God desires to assist us. Our task is to always keep in mind that help is just one prayer away.

God has appointed Himself as the captain of our lives, always present and faithful, never leaving or forsaking us. So, in times of trouble, we must remember to **PRAY THROUGH IT**, knowing that God is ready and willing to guide and protect us.

"If We Pray God Will Answer." – Shavaunta Harris

In every aspect of your life, seek God's guidance first. Ephesians 6 reminds us that we cannot achieve anything through our own efforts alone. Victory comes through prayer and reliance on the spirit. Spiritual forces respond not to human voices, but to the voice of God. Daniel's example illustrates why our prayers may encounter delays; it took 21 days for his prayer to be answered. Those who neglect praying may find themselves empty-handed. Prayerlessness is a plague that leads many believers to blame and drift away from God, when in fact, it is their lack of prayer and persistence that hinder answers. Spiritual forces aim to block answers, which only prayers can overcome.

We dwell on earth but pray from a heavenly perspective. Prayer sustains us supernaturally and enables us to endure, as seen when Aaron's arms were upheld in battle. Prayer is not wishful thinking; it is an act of faith rooted in assurance.

We pray from our heavenly position in Christ, believing it is already complete. Without prayer, we may not realize our lack of power until we need it, as seen when the disciples could not heal a boy due to their faith and abilities rather than God's.

God reigns in the throne of my heart, and no move of God occurs without prayer. Fasting, coupled with prayer, brings deliverance, and connects heaven to earth. Through fasting, we deny ourselves to draw closer to God, but neglecting prayer and fasting can hinder intimacy with Him. God desires to reveal His power through prayer and obedience, as seen in Jesus's ministry.

"Prayer is not just discipline; it's an expression of faith in what's available." – Shavaunta Harris

Struggles In Prayer

Why is it that people find it hard to pray or have difficulty cultivating a prayer life? As we evaluate our prayer lives, it is crucial to explore why we may struggle with praying or feel that our prayers go unanswered. I recently conducted a survey among various groups of believers to understand their perspectives on prayer. I would like to share the findings of this personal study with you. If you have ever doubted the importance of prayer or felt discouraged because you believed your prayers did not matter, you are not alone. I do not want to provide just my own insights, but also the perspectives of others who have encountered similar challenges in prayer.

Here are testimonies from fellow men and women of God who have graciously shared their experiences and offered insight into why some individuals struggle to pray or believe their prayers are ineffective.

Testimonial 1

"One of the reasons people struggle in prayer is that some see God as such a high being beyond their reach. Some may feel that they do not have what it takes to pray to God. Some may ask what should I say to God in prayer? "If only one would draw nigh to God in prayer; God would surely draw nigh to them." James 4:8 - Draw nigh to God, and he will draw nigh to you. If one would say such simple words to God: "Lord teach me how to pray", God will do just that! "Trust in the Lord with all thine heart; and lean not unto thy own understanding. In all thy ways acknowledge him, and he shall direct thy paths." Proverbs 3:5-6

The second reason some struggle in prayer is they do not feel like they are worthy enough to go to God in prayer; due to mistakes, experiences, or unwise choices. If one only knew:

1 John 1:9 – "If we confess our sins, he is faithful and just to forgive us our sins, and to cleanse us from all unrighteousness."

Another reason some struggle when praying to God is their lack of knowledge and understanding. Hosea 4:6 - "My people are destroyed for lack of knowledge." God loves mankind so much, and desires fellowship and communion with Him in prayer. In prayer, there are numerous answers, mysteries, God's purpose, and God's will that He can freely reveal in the place of prayer to mankind. Psalm 16:11 "Thou wilt show me the path of life: in thy presence is fullness of joy; at thy right hand there are pleasures forevermore."

What helped me in the place of prayer is one day I was in fellowship with God and He opened up my understanding about prayer. The spirit of God revealed to me that God is not just my Creator, and Lord and Savior, but God is my Heavenly Father! Once I understood that God is my Heavenly Father. I felt even closer to Him. I began to understand that I am in a relationship with God, and He is my Father who genuinely loves and cares for me beyond my biological father. I began to feel more comfortable and confident that I can go to my Heavenly Father about any and everything, because I am in relationship with God. 2 Corinthians 6:18 - "And will be a Father unto you, and ye shall be my sons and daughters, saith the Lord Almighty."

Once one's understanding opens in the place of prayer; it does not matter what you have done in the past or present that can keep you from confidently going to God in prayer. For God is not just your Creator, Lord, and Savior, but can be your Heavenly Father! Isaiah 53:5 - "But he was wounded for our transgressions, he was bruised for our iniquities: the chastisement of our peace was upon him; and with his stripes we are healed!"

~ Melissa Blacken

Testimonial 2

"God will give you the mind of Christ to understand His heart

Most believers hit a wall & do not know what to say because the exercising of faith has been dormant. God says it is impossible to please Him without faith and if faith is the catalyst to prayer, why do people find it hard to pray or struggle to cultivate a consistent prayer life? Faith and not exercising it or doubting God because of the current circumstances of life. We live in a time where most want prayers answered immediately so most will give up and doubt that prayer works. Prayer outside of the will of God consisting of marriage & ministry should always have the patience to wait on God's direction.

James 5:15 says, it is the prayer of faith, notice how faith and prayer are attached to one another as a husband & wife. It is not the name that the wife takes of her husband that becomes the evidence that they are one, it was the action of saying "I do" and knowing that there was a verbal agreement and action that took place for it to become a manifestation of the act of being together. They both had to be present for the marriage to become a reality with the ordaining minister present. They both had to be consistent on getting to the altar with all the distractions that took place prior to the marriage.

There are other times where believers struggle because of condemnation and not knowing how to separate convictions from the past. Oftentimes I have heard many who have backslid or fell to sin find it hard to go forward because of the previous sin committed so they confuse God's grace with the people's voice. Let us be clear, the Bible never said there was a sinners prayer (John 9:31). God does not hear sinners, but He hears repentance.

Many have gotten caught within the battle of condemnation because of the thought process God does not love me anymore which is something that is further from the truth. In John 11:40-44, Jesus did not raise Lazarus from the dead so that we could see just a miracle. He raised Lazarus from the dead to reveal God's Glory to us by way of faith and to show how God hears us when our hearts are pure and filled with love. Verse 41 Father, I thank thee that you have heard me. Verse 42 and look how faith and he knows God hears him (always).

It's not that God doesn't hear us when we pray but faith must be present like a husband & wife are at the altar when the vows are exchanged with action.

When we do not see things happen right away, it could be faith is not present with prayer, condemnation has taken the place of God's grace, or we just refuse to exercise our prayer life outside of our needs instead of our love for loving God."

~Apostle Brian Lewis Sr., Restoration Kingdom Ministries

Testimonial 3

"It has been, and to be honest, still is currently, one of the most challenging seasons in the area of prayer for me personally...

There is so much authority, victory, and strength accessed When we as God's people come into his presence in prayer! Next to the shed blood of Jesus, it is the greatest gift God has given us is this access!! And because of that, it is also our hardest fought area by the adversary... greatest place of victory and greatest battleground!

Looking back over my life and thinking about the difficult times I have experienced in prayer and why, made me feel like the most wisdom could be gained by looking at the most victorious seasons of my life in the area of prayer and seeing what was different and what I was doing differently where there seemed to be a greater ease of access into His presence and more consistency in prayer...something the Lord showed me the end of spring, early summer this year was "focus gives you greater vision." This came towards the end of a Daniel Fast...and pretty consistently and honestly, I must admit my most victorious and focused seasons in prayer were when I was fasting or in seasons of fasting.

At this point in my life, after walking with the Lord for many years, I feel like I have physically trained myself to either get up early or consistently participate in some kind of prayer call through the week. But what I am noticing, even in those times, I find myself very "absent" in my spirit. The other day, I got up to do devotions, but was unfocused and I cried out to the Lord, "Lord I do not want to get up early in the morning's to be alone with my own thoughts. Lord, I want to be alone with YOU!"

So as much as I hate to admit it, I do believe fasting is one of the greatest tools we have to aid in prayer! Fasting disciplines the body, brings mental focus, spiritual mindedness (greater vision), and spiritual hunger!"

~Pastor Lesley Bradley, Celebrate Love Church

Testimonial 4

"Some reasons I believe people do not cultivate a prayer life are: They have the wrong concept of God; they'll pray and reach out to Him in times of trouble but when things are going well, in their minds, they don't need God anymore (they're more self-reliant than God-dependent). This way of being shows a lack of intimate relationship with God. Some people do not pray because they do not understand God's "ways." They may understand God's acts (things He is capable of doing), however, they do not understand His ways (how God does things which are much higher than human's).

Remember, too, scripture asks, Who can understand the mind of God. (1 Cor. 2:12-16)

Another reason I believe people do not cultivate a prayer life is because they do not go deeper in relationship with God through worship. When Peter was jailed, he was not only praying but he was singing; "singing" denotes the worshiper's heart that goes with prayer. Some do not pray because they lack understanding of the mandate in Genesis 1:26 supporting the necessity of prayer. Because God gave humans dominion/control of the earth, it is our responsibility to rule, and prayer invites God into that responsibility He gave us! God works through humans...even departing the red sea, God worked through a human.

God's word declared and established a spiritual LAW that humans would rule, and God will not violate His established word; therefore, prayer is crucial for the man-God rulership. Prayers carry it out, but few people really understand this. There are more common reasons like people are afraid, they do not know what to say, or they have not been taught."

~Gloria Terry, Founder of Grace Academy of Small Wonders

Testimonial 5

"Do not think God hears them.

- Guilt over a sinful life.

- Comparison with another's prayer life or prayer style (does not match their own).

- The care of life takes priority.

- Do not see immediate results.

- Do not understand what prayer is.

- Do not want God's help."

~Minister Shelbra Woolridge

As highlighted earlier, there are numerous reasons why we may struggle with prayer or feel hesitant to engage in it. In sharing my own struggles with maintaining a consistent prayer life, I want you to know that you are not alone in the journey of growing in fellowship and communion with God. As you read the testimonies and insights of the men and women of God shared above, it is clear that we are all on a journey toward deeper communion with Him.

However, a common misconception is underestimating the power of prayer, especially our authority within it. As believers, we have direct access to God and a supernatural authority bestowed upon us by a supernatural God. Through prayer, we have the ability to bind, loose, cast down, command, declare, and decree from a position of heavenly authority. Prayer is indispensable—it is like oxygen for the soul. Without a prayer life, believers may find it challenging to navigate the spiritual landscape.

Jesus serves as the ultimate example of wielding authority in prayer, as seen in many of His miracles, which were rooted in His deep communion with the Father. One of the clearest examples is the resurrection of Lazarus in John 11:41-44. Before raising Lazarus from the dead, Jesus prayed, thanking the Father for hearing Him.

He said, "Father, I thank you that you have heard me. I knew that you always hear me, but I said this for the benefit of the people standing here, that they may believe that you sent me."
(John 11:41-42, NLT)

This passage highlights Jesus' unwavering confidence in His relationship with the Father and His understanding of the authority He had been given. He spoke directly to Lazarus with the command, "Lazarus, come out!" (John 11:43, NLT), demonstrating the power of authoritative prayer that flows from alignment with God's will. Jesus revealed in this passage just how important it is as children of God to believe Him at his word. When we come to God come believing that He hears us and through that faith trust that He will answer. Come to God with faith and expectation and watch Him move in your situation.

"Comfort zones are an enemy of our prayer life. There is nothing that you haven't already experienced within your comfort zone but so much more to experience beyond them when you pray to God." – Shavaunta Harris

---

10 Practical Tools For Growing In Prayer

1. **Pray The Scriptures:**

   God's word is powerful. He has given us his word to help us navigate through this life. His word instructs us on not only how to pray but how to pray powerful prayers to get a response from God. Praying God's word involves meditating on scripture and using it as the foundation for your prayers. You can start by selecting verses that resonate with your current situation or needs, then personalize them into prayers, expressing your thoughts, feelings, and desires to God based on those scriptures. It is a powerful way to align your prayers with God's will.

   I listed scriptural examples on how to apply this principle in your daily prayer time that can be used as a guide to help you get started.

2. **Prayer For Strength And Guidance:**

   "Lord, your word says in Psalm 32:8, 'I will instruct you and teach you in the way you should go; I will counsel you with my loving eye on you.' Today, I seek your guidance and wisdom in every decision I make. Please lead me and teach me according to your will."

3. **Prayer For Peace And Comfort:**

"Heavenly Father, your word assures me in Philippians 4:6-7, 'Do not be anxious about anything, but in every situation, by prayer and petition, with thanksgiving, present your requests to God. And the peace of God, which transcends all understanding, will guard your hearts and your minds in Christ Jesus.' I surrender my worries and fears to you, and I ask for your peace to fill my heart and mind."

4. **Prayer For Healing And Restoration:**

"Lord, I claim the promise of healing in Isaiah 53:5, 'But he was pierced for our transgressions, he was crushed for our iniquities; the punishment that brought us peace was on him, and by his wounds, we are healed.' I pray for healing and restoration in my body, mind, and spirit. May your healing touch bring wholeness to every part of my being."

5. **Prayer For Strength In Trials:**

"God, your word declares in Romans 8:28, 'And we know that in all things God works for the good of those who love him, who have been called according to his purpose.' Even in the midst of trials and challenges, I trust that you are working for my good. Give me strength and perseverance to endure, knowing that you are with me every step of the way."

6. Prayer For Forgiveness And Renewal:

"Lord Jesus, your word teaches in 1 John 1:9, 'If we confess our sins, he is faithful and just and will forgive us our sins and purify us from all unrighteousness.' I come before you with a repentant heart, asking for your forgiveness and cleansing. Renew me, Lord, and help me walk in obedience to your will."

7. Pray Often

When you are uncertain, just pray. It can be as simple as asking, "Lord, guide my steps today," or "Lord, give me wisdom in this situation." Every aspect of our lives should be covered in prayer. Never stop praying! Jesus set a perfect example in the scriptures by seeking God in every circumstance. We can follow His lead by praying about everything, from mundane to the monumental.

For instance, "Lord, grant me patience in this traffic jam," or "Lord, give me strength to face this challenge." Our relationship with our heavenly Father is primary; it is not just a choice, but a necessity to communicate with Him about every aspect of our lives. Do not relegate prayer to a last resort; make it your foremost and continual pursuit.

- o "Do not be anxious about anything, but in every situation, by prayer and petition, with thanksgiving, present your requests to God." *(Philippians 4:6, NIV)*

74

- "Rejoice always, pray continually, give thanks in all circumstances; for this is God's will for you in Christ Jesus." *(1 Thessalonians 5:16-18, NIV)*

- "The prayer of a righteous person is powerful and effective." *(James 5:16b, NIV)*

8. Make Time

"But seek first his kingdom and his righteousness, and all these things will be given to you as well." *(Matthew 6:33, NIV)*

We meticulously plan our days, from doctor appointments to social gatherings, ensuring every aspect is accounted for. Yet, in the midst of our busy schedules, we often overlook the most important appointment of all: time with God. He deserves not just a place on our schedule, but the topmost priority.

I will admit, I have been guilty of rushing into my day without first spending time with God. But I have learned the hard way that neglecting this vital connection can disrupt my peace and derail my entire day. So, I have made a conscious effort to prioritize God by carving out dedicated time each morning, even before the hustle and bustle begins. If necessary, set reminders or mark it on your calendar, but make sure that fellowship with God takes first place in your life.

9. Be Intentional

"Watch and pray so that you will not fall into temptation. The spirit is willing, but the flesh is weak." *(Matthew 26:41)*

Let's face it, we often have the intention, the desire, and even the heart posture to pray, but countless distractions and obligations thwart our efforts, leaving us without any actual prayer time. It is crucial to carve out dedicated time to pray and seek God.

I recall a period when my prayer life was stagnant and ineffective. I soon realized that I had lost the discipline and focus of intentional prayer. I had neglected the practice of seeking God first thing in the morning, instead rushing into His presence with a laundry list of requests without truly connecting intimately with Him. I had forsaken my intentional pursuit of His presence, and it showed. God has a way of allowing us to run on empty until we are compelled to seek Him earnestly in the secret place for the renewal and refreshment we desperately need.

Towards the end of 2019, I felt spiritually drained, distant from God, and my prayers hit a wall. For those experiencing a similar struggle, let me clarify:

God has not moved; it is us who have shifted our focus, placing other things before Him, thus feeling His distance. I learned that I could not sustain myself on the superficial prayer life I observed in others. God was calling me to deeper intimacy in prayer and devotion, but I hesitated to sacrifice my comfort.

However, remaining in that comfortable yet spiritually stagnant state would have led to my spiritual demise. You cannot afford to linger in a lazy, lackluster prayer life when God is calling you deeper into intimacy with Him. It may require disrupting your schedule, sacrificing sleep, separating yourself, and saying "no" to distractions. But I assure you, it is worth it. You will not survive on the surface level of prayer; it is time to yield to God's call for a more intentional prayer life.

10. Pray Not Always Asking But Thanking Him Only

"Give thanks in all circumstances; for this is God's will for you in Christ Jesus." *(1 Thessalonians 5:18, NIV)*

I recall a friend once telling me that God does not desire a child who constantly begs and cries for what they want but fails to express gratitude when they receive it. As a parent myself, I would not find that attitude appreciable in my own children. Just imagine how God feels about it. What if God only supplied our needs based on what we thanked Him for? Would we have our basic necessities? Would we have food, clothing, or even the ability to perform simple tasks like walking, swallowing, or blinking? We often take these things for granted, failing to appreciate God's grace.

We need to cultivate a habit of gratitude in our prayers. Take time to simply tell God thank you, even for the insignificant blessings. It is not enough to offer occasional thanks; we should live in a perpetual state of gratitude for all He has done. Our God deserves more than sporadic thanksgiving; He deserves a life of continuous gratitude. Take a moment now, pause in your reading, and thank Him.

Reflect on the times when you did not know how ends would meet, when you worried about your child's future, when you felt trapped in an abusive relationship, or when you faced uncertainty about the next day. Yet, despite it all, God provided. Thank Him for His faithfulness and provision.

These are just a few examples; however, you can pray any scripture that speaks to your heart and situation. The key is to personalize (when I say personalize I do not mean change the scripture to fit your situation but align your prayers with the word of God) the verses and make them a heartfelt expression of your desires and needs before God so that your prayers align with his will.

Store Up Treasure In Heaven

"Don't store up treasures here on earth, where moths eat them and rust destroys them, and where thieves break in and steal. Store your treasures in heaven, where moths and rust cannot destroy, and thieves do not break in and steal. Wherever your treasure is, there the desires of your heart will also be." *(Matthew 6:19-21)*

When Scripture speaks of "storing up treasures in heaven," it is referring to investing in spiritual riches rather than earthly wealth. This concept is highlighted in several passages in the Bible, particularly in the teachings of Jesus Christ.

1. **Matthew 6:19-21 (NLT):** In this passage, Jesus instructs his followers not to store up treasures on earth, where they can be destroyed or stolen, but to store up treasures in heaven, where they are secure and lasting. He emphasizes that where your treasure is, your heart will be there also. This suggests that our priorities and affections should be focused on heavenly treasures rather than earthly possessions.

2. **Luke 12:33-34 (NLT):** Jesus advises His disciples to sell their possessions and give to the poor, thereby providing themselves with purses that will not wear out, with a treasure in heaven that will never fail, where no thief comes near, and no moth destroys.

Again, He emphasizes that where your treasure is, your heart will be also.

3. **Matthew 19:21 (NLT):** When Jesus instructs the rich young ruler to sell his possessions and give to the poor in order to have treasure in heaven, He highlights the importance of sacrificing earthly wealth for the sake of eternal rewards.

The detailed meaning of "storing up" treasure in heaven involves several key aspects:

1. **Prioritizing Eternal Values:** It entails valuing spiritual growth, righteousness, love, compassion, and service to others over material wealth and worldly success. It is about aligning our lives with God's kingdom values rather than the fleeting desires of this world.

2. **Investing in Kingdom Work:** Storing up treasures in heaven involves investing our time, talents, and resources in activities that advance God's kingdom on earth. This includes sharing the Gospel, serving others, ministering to the needy, and participating in God's redemptive work in the world.

3. **Seeking Eternal Rewards:** It involves living with an eternal perspective, recognizing that our actions and choices in this life have eternal consequences.

While earthly wealth and possessions are temporary, heavenly treasures are eternal and provide lasting rewards in the presence of God.

4. **Cultivating Spiritual Fruit:** Storing up treasures in heaven also involves cultivating spiritual fruit such as love, joy, peace, patience, kindness, goodness, faithfulness, gentleness, and self-control (Galatians 5:22-23). These qualities reflect the character of Christ and are evidence of a life lived in obedience to God.

In essence, storing up treasures in heaven means living in a way that honors God, serves others, and prioritizes eternal values over temporal pursuits. It is about investing our lives in pursuits that have lasting significance and eternal impact, rather than being consumed by the transient pleasures and possessions of this world.

CHAPTER 3

HOW DO WE PRAY?

It is frequently asked how we pray and not just pray in general but pray effectively. People desire for God to hear them and respond. When confronted with this question, I often emphasize that it is less about the technique of praying and more about the content of our prayers. God is not concerned about the specific method of prayer but rather that we engage in prayer not just with our words but our heart being clean before Him and with His word. He desires to know what is in our hearts, what we desire from Him, and if we are open to understanding His desires for us.

Consider it this way: How did you begin your relationship with your spouse or best friend? Chances are, it involves spending time together and constant communication. Similarly, our Heavenly Father desires that kind of relationship with us. Just as we nurture and develop relationships with those closest to us, we must do the same with God. He longs for us to know Him deeply.

What many may not realize is that God created us for close contact and constant communion with Him. Think of it like this: We raise our children to trust us. When a baby is born, they do not have inherent trust; it is something that develops over time as we consistently care for them and meet their needs. God desires to build that trust with us, meeting our needs and nurturing a strong line of communication between us.

So, open your mouth. Right now! If you have never prayed before, start by simply talking to God as if you were talking to a friend. Be open and honest with God and tell Him what you need. It could involve spending more time in worship without saying much, bearing your burdens and hardships to Him, it could be a crying out for a loved one, or it could be asking God to help you in your prayer journey.

Pray The Word of God

In times when we are uncertain of what to pray for or lack the words, we can turn to the Lord and pray His Word. By identifying scriptures relevant to our situation and lifting them up in prayer, we align ourselves with God's purposes. Throughout the Bible, God's people prayed Scripture, and Jesus Himself frequently prayed according to the Scriptures. It is essential for us to be familiar with the Word in order to pray effectively. **This is the most important principle in this book when it comes to praying effectively.** God responds to His word, and we must pray His word to see results in our prayer life.

Praying Scripture glorifies our heavenly Father, demonstrating our reverence for His Word and His authority in our lives. When we pray, it is vital to align our prayers with the Word of God, rather than solely relying on our emotions or personal inclinations. In Jeremiah 1:12, God reassures Jeremiah that He actively oversees His word to fulfill it. When we pray using the words of Scripture, it is as if we are sending up a signal to the Lord.

Praying the Word positions us as a target for God's attention, much like a flare on the ground signaling a motorist in need of help. I want to stress the importance of this point in prayer.

Whenever praying for anyone our prayers should be littered with the Word of God. The way to ensure you are praying effective prayers is to always pray the Scriptures.

Speaking God's word back to Him establishes a connection between our faith and our prayers. It says to God we believe Him at His Word, and we trust that He is in full control. It grants us access to God's will for our lives. Reflect on how God spoke His Word at the beginning of creation in Genesis chapter one, and how His spoken Word brought about tangible manifestations in the physical realm. When we speak His Word and follow the principles we should expect a response.

This is the key to effective prayer. Praying God's Word to Him assures that you pray God's will. There is nothing more effective in your prayer time than praying the scriptures back to God.

Here are six examples on how you can incorporate verses from the Bible into your prayers:

1. **Choose a Passage:** Select a scripture that speaks to your heart or aligns with your current circumstances. This could be a Psalm, a promise, a command, or a story.

2. **Read and Reflect:** Meditate on the chosen passage. Understand its context and meaning. Reflect on how it applies to your life and situation.

3. **Personalize the Scripture:** Turn the scripture into a prayer by personalizing it. Replace pronouns with your name or the names of others you are praying for, and adapt the language to fit your needs.

4. **Pray the Scripture:** Speak the scripture back to God, making it your prayer. For example, if you are praying Psalm 23, you might say, "Lord, you are my shepherd, I lack nothing. Thank you for making me lie down in green pastures and leading me beside quiet waters."

5. **Use Scripture in Different Prayer Type:** Incorporate scripture into several types of prayer—thanksgiving, confession, petition,

intercession, and praise. Let the words of the Bible guide and shape your prayers.

6. **Be Consistent:** Make praying scripture a regular part of your prayer life. Over time, you will find it becomes more natural and deeply enriching.

Praying scripture will deepen your relationship with God, align your prayers with His will, and provide comfort and guidance through His Word.

Pray With Expectation

Pray with expectation. When we approach prayer, we should come with the conviction that what we are asking for is already accomplished. We enter into prayer with the assurance that God can and, if it aligns with His will, He will respond. Our approach to prayer should be grounded in faith. As mentioned earlier, one of the prerequisites for answered prayers is faith. The Bible teaches us that without faith, it is impossible to please God, and all things are possible for those who believe. Throughout His Word, God repeatedly instructs us to expect Him to fulfill His promises when we pray. He is not a man who would deceive or fail us; His record is one of consistent faithfulness.

Praying with expectation means believing God for the impossible, trusting Him for things our eyes have not yet seen, and relying on His intervention even when circumstances seem dire. It is about facing innumerable challenges, daunting diagnoses, or relentless adversity with unwavering faith. God is moved by our faith and confidence in Him. Just as we seek encouragement from those who believe in us when tackling a task, our expectation moves God's heart and hand.

If our prayers go unanswered, lack of expectation may be a root cause. By praying without expecting God to act, we remove Him from the equation before we even ask. I pray that as you read this chapter, your anticipation of God's faithfulness is reignited. Reflect on all the instances in the Bible where God never failed, not once.

Read the scriptures to meditate on and reflect on the truth of His Word. As believers, we must elevate our expectations of God. He is not like man. He operates on a level far beyond human failures. His Word is steadfast and trustworthy, unlike any promises made by human beings.

So, let us pray with fervor, authority, and anticipation. Each of us has a unique cry and a unique connection with God. Embrace that intimacy in prayer and let your expectation ignite the fire of faith within you.

Pray The Will of God

We must align our prayers with the Father's will. It is crucial for us to pray according to God's will, but to do so, we must understand what His will entails. It is not just about His will for the world but also His will for our lives, relationships, families, finances, and every aspect of our existence. We need to grasp God's intentions not only for the world, but also for our personal lives.

Every day, from the moment we wake up, we should engage in fellowship and communion with God, seeking His desires for us, all for His glory. Our prayers should reflect the mind of God, and we achieve this by discerning His thoughts and seeking His plans through prayer and studying His Word. Praying the will of God means praying the Word of God or praying the scriptures.

Often, our prayers go unanswered, not because God does not hear us or because we are praying incorrectly, but because we are not aligning our prayers with the Father's will. Each of us has a divine purpose ordained by God, and that purpose will be fulfilled. Sometimes, we pray fervently for things that were never meant for us, and thus they never come to fruition. It is not sufficient to just pray; we must pray purposefully in alignment with the Father's will.

Jesus exemplified this perfectly on His way to the cross. In the garden, He prayed, "Father, if it is Your will, take this cup away from Me; nevertheless, not My will, but Yours, be done." Despite facing overwhelming circumstances, Jesus prioritized being in the Father's will more than anything else. Though it may have caused Him pain, His ultimate desire was to fulfill the Father's will. Likewise, our prayer should echo the sentiment: "Not my will, but Yours be done."

Scriptures To Focus On:

- "Your kingdom come, your will be done, on earth as it is in heaven." *(Matthew 6:10, NIV)*

- "This is the confidence we have in approaching God: that if we ask anything according to his will, he hears us." *(1 John 5:14, NIV)*

- "Do not conform to the pattern of this world, but be transformed by the renewing of your mind. Then you will be able to test and approve what God's will is—his good, pleasing and perfect will." *(Romans 12:2, NIV)*

- "The Lord is close to all who call on him, yes, to all who call on him in truth." *(Psalm 145:18, NIV)*

Pray With Intent

Being intentional in prayer means approaching it with purpose and deliberation, aiming for a specific target. In Hebrew, the word *paga* conveys the idea of meeting, encountering, or hitting the mark. When we pray we can be assured that we hit our mark by starting off with a "target" in mind. That target could be a prayer list of people we want to pray for, a scripture or two that we have written down that directs our prayers to God's attention , or by having a topic you want to cover (i.e., children, marriage, or leadership).

We know we will not always come to God in this way but there will be times in your walk with God that you will need to write down your prayer focus. As we take on this mindset *paga* (hitting the mark) it is like your picking up your bow in the spirit, loading it with an arrow, pulling back and hitting the bullseye every time. When we pray the Word of God, we align our prayers with His will, directing our requests in a way that invites His response.

Scripture emphasizes the importance of intentional prayer. In James 5:16, we are encouraged to "confess your sins to each other and pray for each other so that you may be healed. The prayer of a righteous person is powerful and effective." This highlights the effectiveness of targeted, deliberate prayer, especially when offered by those who walk in righteousness.

Additionally, Ephesians 6:18 instructs us to "pray in the Spirit on all occasions with all kinds of prayers and requests. With this in mind, be alert and always keep on praying for all the Lord's people." This verse highlights the need for intentional and continual prayer, covering various aspects of our lives and the lives of others.

It is crucial to avoid praying aimlessly or with a laundry list of requests. Instead, we should seek to discern God's will and pray accordingly. When we enter into our time of prayer with the Lord we should be asking, "Lord what's on your heart, what should I pray about?" Romans 12:2 reminds us, "Do not conform to the pattern of this world, but be transformed by the renewing of your mind. Then you will be able to test and approve what God's will is—his good, pleasing and perfect will."

Praying in alignment with God's will requires commitment and a heart open to His leading. As we cultivate a habit of prayer and immerse ourselves in His Word, we grow in our understanding of His will. Proverbs 3:5-6 assures us, "Trust in the Lord with all your heart and lean not on your own understanding; in all your ways submit to him, and he will make your paths straight."

Therefore, let us approach prayer with intentionality, seeking to align our petitions with God's desires and trusting in His wisdom and guidance. Through intentional prayer, we invite God to work powerfully and effectively in our lives and in the lives of others.

Pray In Unity

In unified prayer, extraordinary things occur. The power of God is unleashed, shattering the darkness of the enemy. Unified prayer opens the heavens, allowing the glory of God to descend. I can personally attest to the transformative power of unified prayer, as it propelled me into the presence of God and filled me with the Holy Spirit.

I recall the profound experience of being baptized and led to a room filled with fervent women of faith, devoted to the power of unified prayer. In the midst of fervent intercession, I felt as though I was wrestling in the spiritual realm, contending with the remnants of my past and the emerging new creation within me. The words of Romans 6:6-8 stirred deeply within me, affirming that my old self had been crucified, and a new identity was beginning to rise.

Amidst the internal struggle, a voice of doubt attempted to dissuade me, filling my mind with fear and hesitation. Yet, amidst the turmoil, a sister in Christ spoke words of affirmation, dispelling the darkness of doubt. In that moment, the battle within ceased, and I surrendered to the divine work of the Holy Spirit. Instantly, His presence fills me, and my tongue was loose to speak in spiritual tongues.

This profound encounter exemplifies the power of unified prayer. Through the collective faith of believers, barriers are broken, and spiritual breakthroughs occur. As Matthew 18:19-20 declares, where two or three gather in agreement, God is present, and His promises are fulfilled. Acts 4:31 recounts how prayer shook the meeting place and filled the believers with boldness. Similarly, Acts 16:25-26 describes how prayer and praise led to a seismic manifestation of God's power, liberating captives. Acts 12:5-12 illustrate how the earnest prayers of the Church brought about miraculous interventions.

Throughout Scripture, the pattern is clear: where unity in prayer exists, the presence and power of God are tangibly felt. As believers gather in unity, the glory of God descends, bringing forth miraculous manifestations. Therefore, let us unite in prayer, expecting divine encounters and supernatural breakthroughs, for the power of unified prayer knows no bounds.

Pray In Faith

We must approach prayer with unwavering faith. The Bible unequivocally states that without faith, it is impossible to please God (Hebrews 11:6). Our faith should not merely exist as a concept but should permeate every aspect of our lives. Scripture urges us to live by faith (Hebrews 10:38) and walk by faith (2 Corinthians 5:7), emphasizing the fundamental role faith plays in our Christian journey.

When we pray, we do so with the conviction that our requests will be granted, for Jesus Himself assures us that whatever we ask for in faith, we will receive (Matthew 21:22). As believers, our entire existence is anchored in faith. The essence of salvation lies in our confession of faith in Jesus Christ and belief in His resurrection (Romans 10:9-10).

Faith empowers us to persistently pray, even in the absence of tangible evidence, trusting that our prayers will yield results. It serves as our offering to God and a precursor to the manifestation of our desires. The book of Hebrews defines faith as the substance of things hoped for and the evidence of things unseen (Hebrews 11:1), highlighting its pivotal role in our spiritual journey.

As we pray, we align our petitions with God's will, confident that He hears and answers us (1 John 5:14). In our daily lives, we often exercise faith without even realizing it. Whether it is praying for the reliability of a worn-out vehicle or seeking provision for financial needs, faith should permeate our every plea.

I urge you to recognize the power of faith when attached to prayer. Activate your faith as you intercede for your needs and desires, knowing that God honors the faith-filled prayers of His children. Trust in His faithfulness, and let your prayers be saturated with unwavering belief in His power to answer.

Ask, Seek, Knock

"And I say unto you, Ask, and it shall be given you; seek, and ye shall find; knock, and it shall be opened unto you. For every one that asketh receiveth; and he that seeketh findeth; and to him that knocketh it shall be opened." *(Luke 11:9-10)*

In the book of Matthew, we see the beginning of Jesus' ministry. He went about all of Galilee, teaching and preaching the Gospel of the kingdom and healing all kinds of sickness and disease among the people. Among those He taught were his disciples. He taught them how to love their enemies, how to please God, how to fast, how to have faith in God, and most importantly He taught them how to pray.

In Luke chapter 11, the disciples were able to see Jesus praying. After witnessing His prayer time, something was stirred within one of His disciples and he makes this statement: "Lord teach us to pray, as John also taught his disciples" (Luke 11:1). What I have often wondered is why did the disciples, of all things, did they ask Jesus to teach them how to pray? In the previous chapters, the disciples had seen Jesus heal the sick, pray, preach to the masses, cast out unclean spirits, and restore the broken.

Of all the things that the disciples saw Jesus do, the lesson they asked of Him was to teach them how to pray. This intrigued me and while searching the scriptures, I strongly believe that the reason that the disciples asked for Jesus to teach them how to pray was because they got the revelation that none of what Jesus had done for the sick, the widow, the demonically possessed, and the feeding of the five thousand could happen without prayer. They understood that if Jesus could do all that He was doing it was not because of the things they saw but because of the power behind the miracles. That power comes from prayer. Jesus' life was proof that prayer was the fuel that empowered Him to do miracles.

If we take a look at the scriptures we will see that Jesus always went away to pray.

- "After He had sent the crowds away, He went up on the mountain by Himself to pray; and when it was evening, He was there alone." *(Matthew 14:23)*

- "After bidding them farewell, He left for the mountain to pray." *(Mark 6:46)*

- "It was at this time that He went off to the mountain to pray, and He spent the whole night in prayer to God." *(Luke 6:12)*

- "In the morning, while it was still dark, Jesus got up, left the house, and went away to a secluded place, and was praying there." *(Mark 1:35)*

- "But Jesus Himself would often slip away to the wilderness and pray." *(Luke 5:16)*

Jesus left a clear path to the power source. He did not leave us guessing or wondering how or where His power came from. When looking at the above scriptures we see Jesus did everything with a heart to please the Father and He did so through the vein of prayer. Jesus gives us a great example of the power of prayer and how to pray.

Jesus taught his disciples the key to answered prayer is asking, seeking, and knocking. We should do so with faith to believe that what we ask in prayer; according to His will, our prayers will be answered. I want to ask you three questions that I believe will help you assess where you are in our prayer life. Are you asking? Are you seeking? Are you knocking?

Luke 11:9-10 says, "And I say unto you, Ask, and it shall be given you; seek, and ye shall find; knock, and it shall be opened unto you. For every one that asketh receiveth; and he that seeketh findeth; and to him that knocketh it shall be opened."

This verse gives us a key to understanding prayer. Have you considered when we read these verses we stress the words "receives, finds, opened?" However, the emphasis in Greek is different. To understand their meaning in English, we have to turn them around: "To receive something, ask! To find something, seek! To get the door open, knock! For everyone who receives has been asking; those who find have been seeking; and those for whom the door is opened have been knocking." When we take a deeper look at the scripture we see that our receiving, finding, and the opening is because we have been consistent in the place of asking, seeking, and knocking.

The same is said about prayer. In order to receive what we are believing God for we have to be praying. In order to see what God has said, we have to have faith and believe it. Prayer is to be a constant in the life of a believer. There is no such thing as "praying when we feel like it." In order to see the answer we must always seek the Father in prayer to stay in alignment with Him and see the fruit of our prayer life.

Now let me make this disclaimer. I am not saying if you pray God will answer every prayer you pray with a "yes." We have to know that God is God. He will do what pleases Him according to His will. Our responsibility is to seek Him in prayer. When we know who our God is we understand that we never stop asking, seeking, or knocking. Our God holds the answers, but He is waiting for us to ask.

Pray Short Prayers

Keep your prayers concise. Often, both new believers and those who have been saved for years think that prayers need to be long and filled with big words to be effective. This kind of thinking will delay some from taking the necessary first step toward building an intimate relationship with God through prayer. However, this could not be further from the truth. Some of the most powerful prayers in the Bible are simple and direct. Jesus gives us notable examples of praying powerful and effective prayers.

Consider these examples of prayer, short yet powerful and effective:

- "Father, forgive them, for they know not what they do." *(Luke 23:34)*
- "Father, into your hands I commit my spirit." *(Luke 23:46)*

Before raising Lazarus, Jesus prayed, "Father, I thank you that you have heard me. I knew that you always hear me, but I said this for the benefit of the people standing here, that they may believe that you sent me." (John 11:41-42)

Upon entering Jerusalem, Jesus prayed, "Now my soul is troubled, and what shall I say? 'Father, save me from this hour'? No, it was for this very reason I came to this hour. Father, glorify your name!" (John 12:27-28)

As we reflect on these scriptures, we see Jesus praying to God for forgiveness for His mockers and executioners. To understand the weight of His words, "Father, forgive them, for they do not know what they are doing" (Luke 23:34), let us consider His physical condition at that moment.

- **Scourging and Beating:** Before the crucifixion, Jesus was scourged, whipped with a *flagrum*— short whip made of at least three leather straps knotted with metal, nails, and bone. This caused deep cuts, severe bruises, and significant loss of blood. He was also beaten, adding more trauma to His body.

- **Carrying the Cross:** After this, Jesus had to carry His cross to Golgotha. Given His injuries, this was incredibly painful and exhausting. The heavy, rough wood added more abrasions and bruises.

- **Nailing to the Cross:** Once at Golgotha, Jesus was nailed to the cross. Iron nails, likely 5-7 inches long, driven through His wrists and feet, causing intense pain by piercing nerves and bones.

- **Hanging on the Cross:** As they raised the cross, the weight of Jesus' body hung from His arms, dislocating His shoulders, and causing extreme pain. Breathing became difficult, requiring Him to push up on His nailed feet and pull up with His arms, leading to severe exhaustion and eventual suffocation.

- **Dehydration and Exposure:** Exposed to the elements and likely dehydrated, His physical suffering was compounded.

- **Blood Loss and Shock:** The cumulative effects of scourging, beating, and crucifixion led to significant blood loss and hypovolemic shock, where the heart struggles to pump blood due to severe fluid loss.

I want you to pause and really take in what you just read. I personally could not imagine enduring that magnitude of pain. In the midst of this brutal suffering, Jesus prayed for forgiveness for those causing His pain. This shows a heart completely submitted to the Father's will. As He was taking His last breath, He used it to pray for the very people who crucified Him. Despite His incomprehensible pain, some of Jesus' final words were used to pray for forgiveness of the very ones who were causing Him unimaginable pain crucifying Him. This is a powerful example for us.

No matter how difficult it gets, we cannot hold back our prayers just because we are going through pain, loss, grief, or persecution. I know it is easier said than done, but these are the very moments where our prayer life deepens. Some of the hardest seasons of my life have become milestones, marking where my prayer life was truly shaped. God longs to hear from us, especially in those times.

Let us follow Jesus' example and live a life of prayer and forgiveness. Remember, by following Jesus' example, we can see that the power of prayer lies not in its length or complexity, but in its sincerity and faith. Keep your prayers simple, direct, and heartfelt, trusting that God hears and understands your every word.

What Does The Bible Say About Prayer?

As we continue to delve into the principles of prayer, we must root ourselves in what the Bible teaches. The Word of God is the foundation of our faith, and it provides clear guidance on how to approach Him in prayer. To have a flourishing and refreshing prayer life, we must go beyond simply knowing about prayer; we must live it. Prayer is not just a spiritual checklist or a tool for emergencies. It's the heartbeat of a thriving relationship with God.

The Bible shows us that prayer is not transactional but relational. Imagine having a friend who only calls when they need something. Over time, that relationship would feel shallow. Similarly, God desires more from us. He longs for deep, meaningful connection—not because of what we can get from Him, but simply because of who He is. John 15:15 reminds us that Jesus calls us friends, not servants, which shows the level of intimacy He desires with us.

When I realized that prayer was more than a "give me" list, my relationship with God changed. I started to see Him as my loving Father, not just a provider. Jesus' death tore the veil, giving us direct access to God (Hebrews 10:19–22). This access is a privilege, and through prayer, we can approach Him with confidence. Hebrews 4:16 tells us to "approach God's throne of grace with confidence, so that we may receive mercy and find grace to help us in our time of need."

Biblical Examples of Prayer

The Bible is filled with examples of individuals who prioritized prayer, showing us what it means to have a vibrant prayer life. These examples teach us to pray honestly, persistently, and with faith:

1. **Hannah's Persistent Prayer (1 Samuel 1:10-20):**
   Hannah's heartfelt prayer for a child shows us the power of pouring out our deepest desires before God. She prayed so fervently that Eli the priest thought she was drunk! Yet God heard her cry and blessed her with Samuel, showing that He honors sincerity and persistence.

2. **David's Honest Prayers (Psalms 51, 23 and more):**
   David's prayers in the Psalms are raw and unfiltered. In times of joy, sorrow, and repentance, David turned to God. Psalm 51 is a beautiful example of repentance, while Psalm 23 expresses trust and comfort in God's guidance.

3. **Jesus' Prayer in Gethsemane (Matthew 26:36-46):**
   Before His crucifixion, Jesus prayed earnestly, asking for God's will to be done, not His own. This moment teaches us that prayer is about surrendering our desires to align with God's plan, even when it's hard.

4. **Paul's Encouragement to Pray:**

(1 Thessalonians 5:17, Philippians 4:6-7)

Paul emphasized constant prayer, urging believers to pray without ceasing and to bring every concern to God with thanksgiving. He knew that prayer was the key to peace.

How Do We Pray?

The disciples asked Jesus this very question, and He gave them the Lord's Prayer as a model (Matthew 6:9-13). This prayer is not just a template but a guide for how to approach God:

- Adoration: "Our Father in heaven, hallowed be your name."
- Submission: "Your kingdom come, your will be done."
- Petition: "Give us today our daily bread."
- Confession: "Forgive us our debts, as we forgive our debtors."
- Protection: "Lead us not into temptation, but deliver us from evil."

Jesus also instructed us not to pray with empty repetition or to impress others (Matthew 6:5-7). Instead, He calls us to pray authentically, trusting that our Father already knows what we need.

Growing In Prayer

Prayer is a journey. At first, it might feel awkward or routine, but as you spend more time with God, it becomes as natural as breathing. Just as any relationship requires time and effort to grow, so does your relationship with God through prayer. Romans 12:12 encourages us to "be joyful in hope, patient in affliction, faithful in prayer." Faithfulness in prayer is key.

God's Word says, "The Lord is near to all who call on him, to all who call on him in truth" (Psalm 145:18). This promise reminds us that God is not distant. He hears us, loves us, and desires to be close to us. So, whether you are celebrating a victory or walking through the valley of despair, turn to Him in prayer. He is ready to listen, ready to comfort, and ready to lead you.

Remember, prayer is not just about asking—it is about aligning. It's not just about speaking—it is about listening. And it is not just about religion—it is about relationship. Let your prayer life become a daily, living connection with the God who created you and loves you beyond measure.

CHAPTER 4

TYPES OF PRAYER

Biblical Intercession and Intercessors

An Intercessor is someone who takes on the burdens and request of God and others, and is willing to lay between the pews and the altar and cry out to the Father for an answer. Biblical intercession is a form of prayer in which one person petitions God on behalf of others. It involves standing in the gap between God and individuals or situations, pleading for God's mercy, guidance, protection, or intervention on behalf of others. Intercessory prayer is deeply rooted in the Bible and is considered a powerful way to advocate for others before God.

In my opinion, intercession, apart from your personal prayer life, is one of the most important postures of prayer. Lives have been transformed, cities have been changed, and laws have been enacted all because someone carried the Lord's burden in prayer. I have personally witnessed the power of intercession move in my life, in the lives of those around me, and even in the lives of strangers.

There is immense value in interceding and praying, as many of the burdens for prayer come directly from God's heart to ours. Whether it is for an individual, a situation, or something happening in our country or in other countries, the intercessor plays a vital role in the lives of every believer.

The Bible instructs us to pray for one another with all kinds of prayers and supplication (Ephesians 6:18). It also tells us to never stop praying (1 Thessalonians 5:17). I passionately believe in the great power of praying for one another. Through intercession, we align our hearts with God's will and bring about His purposes on earth.

An example of biblical intercession is in the book of Genesis, chapters 18 and 19, where Abraham intercedes for the city of Sodom and Gomorrah. The Lord reveals to Abraham that he intends to destroy the cities because of their wickedness.

Concerned for the righteous people living there, Abraham begins to intercede on their behalf:

- In Genesis 18:23-32 (NLT): Abraham approached him and said, "Will you sweep away both the righteous and the wicked? Suppose you find fifty righteous people living there in the city— will you still sweep it away and not spare it for their sakes? Surely you wouldn't do such a thing, destroying the righteous along with the wicked.

  Why, you would be treating the righteous and the wicked exactly the same! Surely you wouldn't do that! Should not the Judge of all the earth do what is right?" And the Lord replied, "If I find fifty righteous people in Sodom, I will spare the entire city for their sake." Then Abraham spoke again. "Since I have begun, let me speak further to my Lord, even though I am but dust and ashes.

- Suppose there are only forty-five righteous people rather than fifty? Will you destroy the whole city for lack of five?" And the Lord said, "I will not destroy it if I find forty-five righteous people there."

Then Abraham pressed his request further. "Suppose there are only forty?" And the Lord replied, "I will not destroy it if there are forty." "Please don't be angry, my Lord," Abraham pleaded. "Let me speak— suppose only thirty righteous people are found?" And the Lord replied, "I will not destroy it if I find thirty. "Then Abraham said, "Since I have dared to speak to the Lord, let me continue—suppose there are only twenty?" And the Lord replied, "Then I will not destroy it for the sake of the twenty." Finally, Abraham said, "Lord, please don't be angry with me if I speak one more time. Suppose only ten are found there?" And the Lord replied, "Then I will not destroy it for the sake of the ten."

Abraham's intercession reveals essential principles of biblical intercession—truths that should live at the core of every intercessor's heart:

1. **Concern for Others:**

   Abraham is deeply concerned about the fate of the righteous people living in Sodom and Gomorrah and pleads with God to spare the cities for their sake.

2. **Boldness in Prayer:**

   Abraham approaches God with boldness, humbly yet persistently advocating for the righteous in the face of impending judgment.

3. **Negotiation with God:**

   Abraham engages in a sort of negotiation with God, proposing different scenarios and asking if God would spare the cities for the sake of a smaller number of righteous people.

4. **Compassion and Mercy:**

   Through Abraham's intercession, we see God's compassion and mercy in considering the plea for the sake of even a few righteous individuals.

Additional Biblical Intercession Examples:

1. **Moses Interceding for Israel:**
   Exodus 32:11-14: When the Israelites made a golden calf, God was ready to destroy them. Moses interceded on their behalf, reminding God of His promises, and God relented from bringing disaster upon His people.

2. **Abraham Interceding for Sodom:**
   Genesis 18:22-33: Abraham pleaded with God to spare Sodom if righteous people could be found there. Though the city was destroyed, Abraham's intercession highlighted the power of standing in the gap for others.

3. **Jesus Praying for Peter:**
   Luke 22:31-32: Jesus told Peter that He had prayed for him so that his faith would not fail. Jesus' intercession for Peter demonstrates the sustaining power of prayer.

4. **Paul's Intercession for the Churches:**

   Ephesians 1:15-18: Paul often prayed for the spiritual growth and enlightenment of the believers in the churches he established, emphasizing the importance of continual prayer for one another.

Biblical intercession involves standing in the gap, pleading for mercy and intervention on behalf of others, and trusting in God's justice and mercy.

My Prayer For Intercessors

Heavenly Father,

We lift up to you all those called to the ministry of intercession. Awaken their hearts from any apathy or complacency. Stir within them a renewed passion for fervent prayer, and may they hear Your voice clearly, drawing them back to their place of intimacy with You. Give them the strength to persevere in prayer, not losing heart, but pressing on with unwavering faith.

Lord, grant them the vision to see beyond the natural and to trust in Your divine plans. May they seek Your face above all else, making You their first pursuit each day. Nourish their spirits with Your Word, filling them with wisdom, understanding, and discernment. Let them clearly hear Your voice and be guided by Your Spirit alone.

We come against any words of judgment or condemnation spoken over their lives, declaring them canceled. Let Your truth and promises stand strong in their hearts, giving them confidence and peace.

Father, we pray for those who have felt discouraged, dry, or distant from You. Remind them of Psalm 77, which assures us that You hear our cries and deliver us in times of trouble. For those struggling to pray or feeling far from You, may they know that You are not condemning them, but lovingly inviting them back into Your presence.

You are a God of grace and compassion, not manipulation or force. You understand our struggles and welcome us back with open arms. For those who have been hurt or wounded, we ask for Your healing touch. Restore them to a place of communion with You, where they can find peace, strength, and renewal.

We trust in Your unfailing love and mercy. Awaken Your intercessors, renew their passion for prayer, and accomplish Your will in their lives.

In Jesus' precious name, we pray,
Amen.

Prophetic Intercession and Intercessors

Prophetic intercession is a form of prayer in which individuals are led by the Holy Spirit to pray for specific people, situations, or events, often with insights that go beyond their natural understanding. Prophetic intercessors play a crucial role in discerning God's will, perceiving spiritual realities, and praying accordingly. The Bible provides several examples of prophetic intercession.

Prophetic Intercessors Scripture Examples:

1. **Daniel**

   Daniel 9:2-3, 20-23: Daniel was a man of deep prayer and intercession. He received prophetic revelations through visions and dreams and prayed accordingly, confessing the sins of Israel and seeking God's mercy and intervention.

2. **Anna**

   Luke 2:36-38: Anna, a prophetess, devoted herself to fasting and prayer in the temple. She received prophetic revelation about the Messiah and spoke about Him to all who were looking forward to the redemption of Jerusalem.

3. **Elijah**

   1 Kings 18:36-39: Elijah, a prophet, interceded on Mount Carmel for God to demonstrate His power and turn the hearts of Israel back to Him. His prayer and prophetic action resulted in a miraculous display of God's power.

4. **Jeremiah**

   Jeremiah 7:16, 11:14 and 14:11: Jeremiah was both a prophet and an intercessor. He received direct revelations from God about the fate of Israel and interceded for the people, though at times God instructed him to stop praying for them due to their persistent disobedience.

Prophetic Intercessor Characteristics

A prophetic intercessor is someone who combines the roles of an intercessor and a prophet. This individual not only prays on behalf of others but also receives divine revelations, insights, and prophetic messages from God that guide their intercession. Prophetic intercessors can also carry the burden of the watchmen and often times many prophets and prophetic people have been called to the watchtower to be watchmen. Identifying whether you have the gift of prophetic intercession involves recognizing certain characteristics and experiences that align with this spiritual calling.

Before discussing the roles and responsibilities of a prophetic intercessor, it's essential to make an important disclaimer. The most crucial aspect of being a prophetic intercessor, is that the individual's life must be fully surrendered to God and the Holy Spirit. This involves consistent time in the Word, dedicated prayer, and accountability to someone who can provide external guidance and correction.

A prophetic intercessor must maintain a personal relationship with God and adhere to a biblical standard of holiness and righteousness. Many may claim the title of a prophetic intercessor without embracing the necessary lifestyle. Therefore, I caution anyone to ensure that the fruit of the Spirit is evident in their life and that they are committed to living righteously as they identify with the characteristics of a prophetic intercessor.

Here are some character traits to help you discern if you might have the gift of prophetic intercession:

1. **Sensitivity to the Spirit:**
   Prophetic intercessors often have a heightened sensitivity to the leading and prompting of the Holy Spirit. They may frequently sense God's presence, nudges, or impressions guiding them in prayer, able to discern His voice and direction clearly.

2. Receiving Revelations:

Prophetic intercessors may receive insights, revelations, dreams, words of knowledge, and other prophetic insights or visions from the Holy Spirit during prayer. These revelations can pertain to specific situations, individuals, or future events, providing guidance for intercession.

3. Burden for Prayer:

Prophetic intercessors often feel a deep burden or urgency to pray for specific issues, regions, or people groups. They may be moved to intercede fervently, even when they do not fully understand the reasons behind their prayers. Prophetic intercessors have a profound and consistent prayer life. They spend significant time in prayer, often interceding on behalf of individuals, groups, or situations as led by the Holy Spirit.

4. Spiritual Discernment:

Prophetic intercessors possess a gift of or keen sense of discernment, enabling them to perceive spiritual realities, the workings of the enemy and underlying issues that may not be visible to others. They can discern between truth and deception, identifying areas of spiritual warfare that require prayer.

5. **Praying in Alignment with Scripture:**

Prophetic intercessors pray in alignment with God's Word, often using Scripture as the foundation for their prayers. They seek to pray according to God's will, speaking His promises and declarations into situations.

6. **Intercessory Crying Out:**

Prophetic intercessors may experience times of intense intercession, where they cry out to God with passion and urgency, often feeling the weight of the burdens they carry in prayer.

7. **Desire for God's Presence:**

Prophetic intercessors have a deep hunger and thirst for God's presence. They prioritize intimacy with God through prayer, worship, and seeking His face, knowing that effective intercession flows from communion with Him.

8. **Confirmation from Others:**

Prophetic intercessors may receive confirmation of their gifting from fellow believers or spiritual leaders who recognize and affirm the prophetic anointing on their prayers.

9. Fruitfulness in Prayer:

Prophetic intercessors often experience tangible results and answers to prayers as a result of their intercession. They may witness breakthroughs, spiritual shifts, and transformations in individuals or situations they have prayed for.

10. Persistent Intercession:

Prophetic intercessors demonstrate persistence in prayer, persevering even when faced with opposition or discouragement. They understand the importance of standing in the gap and contending for God's purposes to be fulfilled.

11. Obedience and Boldness:

Prophetic intercessors are obedient to the revelations and instructions they receive from God, often stepping out in faith to pray or act on these revelations, even when it requires boldness and courage.

12. Spiritual Warfare

They engage in spiritual warfare, praying against spiritual forces of darkness and interceding for protection, deliverance, and breakthrough.

If you resonate with several of these characteristics and experiences, it is possible that you have the gift of prophetic intercession. It is essential to seek confirmation, guidance, from God and mentorship from mature believers and spiritual leaders as you grow and develop in this gift.

Personal Prayer

Personal prayer is the individual act of communicating with God, expressing one's thoughts, emotions, desires, and concerns directly to Him. Here are ten biblical and practical examples of personal prayer:

1. **Morning Devotion:**
   Begin your day by spending time in prayer, seeking God's guidance, and surrendering the day to Him. Jesus often started His day in prayer, as seen in Mark 1:35.

2. **Thanksgiving and Praise:**
   Take time to thank God for His blessings and praise Him for who He is. Psalm 100:4 encourages us to enter His gates with thanksgiving and His courts with praise.

3. **Confession and Repentance:**

Confess your sins and shortcomings to God, asking for His forgiveness and cleansing. 1 John 1:9 assures us that if we confess our sins, He is faithful and just to forgive us.

4. **Seeking Wisdom and Guidance:**

Ask God for wisdom and guidance in making decisions and navigating life's challenges. James 1:5 encourages us to ask God for wisdom, and He will generously give it.

5. **Intercession for Others:**

Lift up the needs of others in prayer, interceding on their behalf. James 5:16 encourages us to pray for one another, as the prayer of a righteous person is powerful and effective.

6. **Strength and Courage:**

Pray for strength and courage to face difficulties and trials. Joshua 1:9 reminds us to be strong and courageous, for the Lord is with us wherever we go.

7. **Protection and Provision:**

   Ask God for protection from harm and provision for your needs. Philippians 4:6-7 encourages us to present our requests to God, and His peace will guard our hearts and minds.

8. **Listening to God's Voice:**

   Spend time in silence, listening for God's voice through His Word, His Spirit, and His leading. Psalm 46:10 instructs us to "be still, and know that I am God."

9. **Gratitude for Answered Prayer:**

   Thank God for answering prayers and for His faithfulness. Psalm 118:21 declares, "I will give you thanks, for you answered me; you have become my salvation."

10. **Seeking His Presence:**

   Long for intimacy with God and seek His presence in prayer. Psalm 27:8 encourages us to seek His face and assures us that He will not hide His face from us.

Personal prayer is a vital aspect of the Christian life, allowing believers to deepen their relationship with God, grow in faith, and experience His presence and power in their lives.

Corporate Prayer

Corporate prayer is when a group of believers come together to pray, lifting their voices in unity before God. Here are nine biblical and practical examples of corporate prayer:

1. **Prayer Meetings:**
   Gatherings specifically designated for prayer, where believers come together to intercede for various needs, individuals, communities, and nations. Acts 1:14 describes the early believers being "together in prayer" in the upper room.

2. **Church Services:**
   Prayer is often a significant component of church services, where congregations join together in prayer for the church, its leaders, the community, and specific needs. Acts 2:42 mentions the early believers devoting themselves to the apostles' teaching and fellowship, including prayers.

3. **Prayer Circles:**
   Small groups or circles of believers who meet to pray for one another, share personal needs, and intercede with specific concerns. Acts 12:12 describe how believers gathered at Mary's house to pray for Peter when he was in prison.

4. **Prayer Walks:**

   Groups of believers walking together through neighborhoods, cities, or specific areas, praying for the people, situations, and needs they encounter. Nehemiah 1:4-6 records Nehemiah's prayer while walking through the streets of Jerusalem, interceding for the city and its people.

5. **Prayer Chains:**

   Networks of believers that commit to pray for specific requests or needs, passing them along to others in the chain. Acts 12:5 mentions believers gathering to pray earnestly for Peter's release from prison.

6. **Concerts of Prayer:**

   Larger gatherings where multiple churches or denominations come together for extended periods of corporate prayer, seeking God's intervention and revival in the region. Acts 4:24-31 records the believers praying together in unity for boldness to proclaim the gospel.

7. **Prayer Vigils:**

   Continuous periods of prayer where believers take shifts to pray throughout the day or night, often in response to urgent needs or crises. Acts 12:12 describe believers gathering for prayer throughout the night when Peter was in prison.

8. **Mission Prayer Groups:**

   Groups of believers who come together to pray specifically for missionaries, mission organizations, and unreached people groups around the world. Romans 15:30-31 encourages believers to join together in prayer to spread of the gospel.

9. **National or Global Prayer Initiatives:**

   Times when believers across a nation or around the world unite in prayer for specific issues, such as repentance, revival, or social justice. 2 Chronicles 7:14 calls for God's people to humble themselves, pray, seek His face, and turn from their wicked ways for national healing.

Corporate prayer is a powerful expression of unity among believers, as they join their hearts and voices together to seek God's will and intervention in various situations and circumstances.

Praying in Tongues

What is it?

Praying in tongues, also known as speaking in tongues, is a spiritual gift where the Holy Spirit enables a believer to pray in a language unknown to them. It is a form of prayer that bypasses human understanding, allowing the Spirit to intercede directly through the believer. This type of prayer connects us to God's Spirit in a deeper way, as the Holy Spirit prays through us, often for things we may not even be aware of.

Why is it important?

Praying in tongues is crucial because it helps us to navigate through prayer more effectively. When we do not know what to pray for or how to articulate our needs, praying in tongues allows the Holy Spirit to intercede on our behalf. This gift enables us to pray exactly what God desires for us, aligning our will with His. It is a way of allowing the Holy Spirit to pray through us when we might not have the words or understanding of a situation.

As Romans 8:26 (NLT) says, "And the Holy Spirit helps us in our weakness. For example, we don't know what God wants us to pray for. But the Holy Spirit prays for us with groanings that cannot be expressed in words." Praying in tongues strengthens our spirit and deepens our communication with God.

What does the Bible say about it?

The Bible teaches that praying in tongues is a gift from the Holy Spirit. In 1 Corinthians 14:2 (NLT), it says, "For if you have the ability to speak in tongues, you will be talking only to God, since people won't be able to understand you. You will be speaking by the power of the Spirit, but it will all be mysterious." This verse highlights that praying in tongues is a direct communication with God, empowered by the Holy Spirit.

Additionally, in 1 Corinthians 14:4 (NLT), it says, "A person who speaks in tongues is strengthened personally..."—demonstrating that this gift is designed to edify and build up the individual spiritually.

How do I pray in tongues?

To pray in tongues, you need to first ask the Holy Spirit to fill you and empower you with this gift. Begin by focusing your heart on God, worshipping, and praising Him. As you open yourself up to the Holy Spirit, allow Him to move through you. The words may not make sense to your mind, but trust that the Holy Spirit is leading your prayer.

Luke 11:13 (NLT) encourages us to ask for the Holy Spirit: "So if you sinful people know how to give good gifts to your children, how much more will your heavenly Father give the Holy Spirit to those who ask him." With faith and openness, you can receive the gift of tongues, allowing the Spirit to guide your prayer life in a powerful way.

The Watchman

Watchmen's ears are at attention to the Father's voice and his alone, true watchmen cry loud and spare not. They carry the burdens of the Father's heart, and they pray according to what the Lord has said and shared with them by the spirit. They have committed to a life of prayer and fasting and likeness to the gift of the prophet. They are the trumpet in the hand of God that warns a God's people of danger, and prays for God's end result. Watchmen must live a life of consecration unto the Lord (Ezekiel 3:17-21). Watchmen also carry a strong gift of discernment.

Biblical Definition of a Watchman

A watchman in biblical terms is someone appointed by God to be vigilant, alert, and responsible for warning others of impending danger, both physical and spiritual. The primary role of a watchman is to stand guard, observe, and sound the alarm when necessary to protect and guide the community.

Here are three biblical examples of a watchman:

1. **Ezekiel**

    "Son of man, I have made you a watchman for the people of Israel; so hear the word I speak and give them warning from me." *(Ezekiel 3:17)*

Ezekiel's role was to receive messages from God and deliver warnings to the people of Israel, urging them to repent and return to God to avoid impending judgment.

2. **Isaiah**

    "For thus the Lord said to me: 'Go, set a watchman; let him announce what he sees.'" *(Isaiah 21:6)*

    Isaiah was instructed to appoint a watchman to observe and report any signs of danger, symbolizing the importance of vigilance and readiness.

3. **Habakkuk**

    "I will stand at my watch and station myself on the ramparts; I will look to see what he will say to me, and what answer I am to give to this complaint." **(Habakkuk 2:1)**

    Habakkuk positioned himself as a watchman to wait for God's message, illustrating the watchman's role in seeking and conveying divine guidance.

Characteristics of a Watchman

1. Characteristics of a Watchman

- o Vigilance: Constantly alert and attentive to spiritual and moral dangers.
- o Responsibility: Feels a deep sense of duty to warn and guide others.
- o Faithfulness: Committed to delivering God's messages accurately and promptly.
- o Discernment: Able to perceive and understand spiritual realities and dangers.
- o Courage: Willing to speak out and warn others, even if it's unpopular or dangerous.

2. How to Identify if You Are a Watchman

- o Spiritual Sensitivity: Do you often feel prompted by the Holy Spirit to warn others of spiritual dangers or guide them towards righteousness?
- o Burden for Others: Do you have a deep concern for the spiritual well-being of your community or loved ones?
- o Prophetic Insight: Do you receive and understand messages from God that need to be communicated to others?

o   Desire to Protect: Are you driven to protect others from harm, both physically and spiritually?

o   Sense of Duty: Do you feel an intense sense of responsibility to speak truth, even when it is difficult?

Five Practical Steps to Embrace the Role of a Watchman

1. Prayer and Study: Regularly seek God's guidance through prayer and studying His Word.

2. Spiritual Discernment: Develop discernment by staying close to God and being sensitive to His voice.

3. Communicate Clearly: When prompted, share God's warnings and guidance with clarity and compassion.

4. Be Courageous: Stand firm in your convictions, even in the face of opposition.

5. Stay Humble: Always rely on God's strength and wisdom, recognizing that you are His servant.

Biblical examples like Ezekiel, Isaiah, and Habakkuk illustrate the roles and characteristics of a watchman. If you possess spiritual sensitivity, a burden for others, prophetic insight, a desire to protect, and a sense of duty, you might be called to be a watchman. Embrace this role through prayer, discernment, clear communication, courage, and humility.

Fasting And Prayer

As we discuss prayer and fasting, I want to be sure that you have a clear understanding of what fasting and prayer is based on biblical examples. I want to stress the importance of a biblical fast. This is especially important because we live in a time where our comfort and picking what we want to surrender to dictates the kind of fast we are willing to participate in. Many have come to see fasting as something based on what we "think" God will accept. As long as it "looks" like we are sacrificing something, then God has to be ok with it, right? Wrong!

We have somehow invented all kinds of unbiblical fast done in the name of God as if God has to accept it. This could not be further from biblical truth of what it means to fast. When discussing prayer and fasting, we are going to take a look at what it means to fast biblically, how to pray and fast biblically and what is the purpose of fasting.

What Is Fasting?

The Greek word for fasting is *nesteia* which means to voluntarily abstain from food or to fast. Fasting is voluntarily abstaining from food (and sometimes drink) for a period to seek God more intently through prayer, repentance, and spiritual focus. To fast means to afflict your soul or self, the practice of self-denial, abstinence from food.

The origins of biblical fasting can be traced back to the early practices of the Israelites in the Old Testament. Some biblical examples are in Exodus 34:28, Leviticus 16:29-31, 1 Samuel 7:6. The origins of biblical fasting are deeply rooted in the practices of the Israelites, where it served as a means of seeking God's guidance, expressing repentance, and showing earnestness in prayer. This practice continued and was refined through the teachings and example of Jesus in the New Testament. Fasting remains a significant spiritual discipline for believers, focused on deepening their relationship with God.

We can see how effective fasting is by the fact that even Satanists recognize its power and use it to their advantage. When we deny ourselves of our natural desires — eating and drinking to draw closer to God, we open ourselves up for our spirit to be cleansed. Abstaining from food also strengthens us as we pray. When you fast, it is not about dieting or losing weight, although those might be side effects. Our focus is solely on seeking the presence of God, His counsel, His wisdom, and His understanding.

Fasting is to be done in secret Matthew 6:16-18. Unless you are participating in a corporate fast, do it according to scripture. During your fasting time you should be seeking the Lord and praying, reading your Bible, and separating yourself from your normal everyday activities.

Prayer and fasting

During your prayer and fasting time, I recommend that you keep some kind of journal or notebook to document what you are hearing from God. Prayer and fasting are synonymous, and you cannot have one without the other. Fasting empties us of our human desires, selfish ways and refocuses our attention on God, His spirit, His desires, and His voice. As we deny ourselves, we empty as He pours and fills us with Him. Our hearing His voice becomes clear.

Fasting helps us to hear and pray to connect us to His will. Prayers empower us to obey what He says to us during our prayer and fasting time. Jesus shows us in scripture that some things we pray for or about, cannot be moved without our prayers accompanied with fasting (Matthew 17:20-21 & Mark 9:28-29).

Reasons for prayer and fasting via scripture reference:

1. **Preparing for ministry:**
   - Jesus' 40 days of prayer and fasting in the wilderness.
   - Paul and Barnabas fasted and prayed before serving in ministry.

2. Seeking God, guidance:

- o Esther fasted, for three days to seek wisdom, discernment protection, and guidance.

- o In Acts 13:2-3 a group of people while worshiping God, fasted and prayed for guidance and the Holy Spirit told them to commission Paul and Barnabas.

- o Moses fasted on the mountain to receive the new tablet and God's explanation of the covenant with the Israelites.

- o Elijah had just confronted the prophets of Baal on Mount Carmel, demonstrating God's power (1 Kings 18). However, Queen Jezebel threatened his life, and in fear, Elijah fled into the wilderness. Overwhelmed and feeling hopeless, Elijah sought God's guidance.

3. Showing grief:

- o Nehemiah learning the condition of Jerusalem's destruction prayed to God, asking for wisdom, understanding and favor. He fasted and mourned when he learned Jerusalem's walls had been broken down.

- o David did a fast and prayed that his child with Bathsheba would live after his affair.

- o The people of Israel mourned for 30 days after Moses' death.

Fasting can be a response to grief and a way to focus on God. The Bible also teaches that mourning can be a pathway to attract blessings from God through fasting and mourning together along with weeping and inward sorrow.

4. **Repenting:**
   o Joel 1:14 God causes people to pray through His prophet to consecrate a fast and set aside time to pray.
   o Nehemiah's prayer included repentance for the sins of Israel and his family, as well as a plea for God's favor to restore Jerusalem after he learned the walls had been broken down (Nehemiah 1:1-11).
   o Solomon prayed that God would forgive the sins of the people and hear the prayers of the people as they pray from the temple. This was his prayer during the dedication of the temple in 1 Kings 8:46-53 and 2 Chronicles 6:36-39.
   o Ezra called a corporate fast and prayed for the Israelite's safe journey.
   o Jonah warned the city of Nineveh. The king ordered the people to fast and repent for three days.
   o The Israelites after losing 40,000 men in battle, the Israelites fasted until evening.
   o David in Psalms 69, expressed his remorse through prayer and fasting.

5. **Expressing longing and love for God:**

   o Prophetess Anna is described as worshiping night and day. She committed to fast and pray unto the Lord. Luke 2:37. She was a woman that devoted herself to fasting, and praying day and night.

   o Joel 2:13 reads: "Don't tear your clothing in your grief, but tear your hearts instead." Return to the Lord your God, for he is merciful and compassionate, slow to get angry and filled with unfailing love. He is eager to relent and not punish."

This translation conveys the same message of focusing on inner repentance rather than outward rituals. This scripture speaks about genuine repentance and transformation. We can also apply repentance to our prayer life. God desires, genuine fasting and prayer unto Him, coupled with repentance that will produce transformation in us. God does not want you to simply reduce your TV time or fast from your morning coffee. He desires for you to present your whole heart and life and not just your actions. Jesus instructed us to fast not for external appearances but for internal transformation.

"Pray beyond what people say because God always has the final say." – Shavaunta Harris

---

What is the Purpose of Fasting and Prayer?

There are many purposes of fasting and prayer. When we look at the Bible we can find many reasons why we fast and pray. Let us survey some of those examples through scripture.

1. **Seeking God's Guidance:**
   Leaning on God and His wisdom is a reason that we take time to pray before making any decisions. God's wisdom isn't like ours and He has a greater perspective of our situation than we do. When we are in a situation that we need insight we fast and pray to be sure that we are led by the spirit. When we pray and fast we seek divine counsel, and not counsel of self or of men. **The early church fasted and prayed before sending out missionaries. (Acts 13:2-3)**

2. **Repentance and Humility:**
   When we have sinned against God we open the door for many spiritual attacks. What we have to understand is that God's word says, a broken spirit and a contrite heart He will not condemn. We need God's help to live a righteous life, and we will have times where we or even our brothers and sisters in the faith may fall.

It is our responsibility to humble ourselves, admit to God that we have sinned, decide to turn from sin and back to God in complete repentance, and then lean on God for the strength to turn from sin. **The people of Nineveh fasted and repented at Jonah's preaching. (Jonah 3:5-10)**

3. **Expressing Grief:**

    Many times, in the Bible we see examples of men and women praying and fasting because of grief. There is time in Judaism during mourning there would be a time of fasting, and prayer called Shiva. The people would take time to seek comfort from God and to mourn. **Nehemiah fasted and prayed upon hearing about Jerusalem's desolation. (Nehemiah 1:4)**

4. **Seeking Deliverance or Protection:**

    Fasting and prayer are imperative during times of spiritual warfare or spiritual attack. It is important to remember that prayer and fasting are a weapon against our enemies when we intentionally fast and pray. **Esther fasted before approaching the king to save her people. (Esther 4:16)**

5. **Spiritual Strengthening:**

    Fasting and prayer builds up our spiritual strength and stamina. We are able to increase in discernment and hear the spirit of God. **Jesus fasted in the wilderness to prepare for His ministry. (Matthew 4:1-11)**

6. **Worship and Devotion:**

   Fasting and prayer is another way to show devotion to God and to worship. Our fasting says to God there is nothing more I want but you and you are the only thing that satisfies me. **Anna the prophetess, worshiped with fasting and prayer in the temple. (Luke 2:37)**

How To Fast And Pray?

How to Fast Biblically

Again, I want to emphasize the importance of taking note that any biblical fast constitutes abstaining from food. There was no one in the Bible staying away from T.V., coffee or social media, but going on a fast means that there is a period of time where we abstain completely from food.

1. **Set Your Purpose:**

   Determine why you are fasting. Common biblical purposes include seeking God's guidance, expressing grief, seeking deliverance or protection, and showing repentance. "So we fasted and petitioned our God about this, and he answered our prayer." *(Ezra 8:23)*

2. **Prepare Spiritually:**

Confess your sins and commit to seeking God during the fast. "When you fast, do not look somber as the hypocrites do, for they disfigure their faces to show others they are fasting." *(Matthew 6:16)*

3. **Choose a Type of Fast:**

Decide the nature of your fast (e.g., total fast, partial fast, abstaining from certain foods). Daniel fasted by eating no meat, wine, or rich foods. (Daniel 10:3)

4. **Focus on God:**

Use the time normally spent eating to pray, read the Bible, and worship. "While they were worshiping the Lord and fasting, the Holy Spirit said..." *(Acts 13:2)*

5. **Break the Fast Gradually:**

When the fast ends, gradually reintroduce food to your diet.

Practical note: Breaking a fast with light foods, like fruits and soups can help your body readjust.

Prayer and fasting are powerful spiritual disciplines that bring believers closer to God. Biblically, they are acts of worship, repentance, and seeking divine guidance. Effective prayer includes adoration, confession, thanksgiving, supplication, and listening. Fasting should be purposeful, spiritually prepared for, and accompanied by focused prayer.

The purposes of fasting and prayer range from seeking guidance and protection to expressing grief and devotion. By understanding and practicing these disciplines biblically, believers can deepen their relationship with God and align their lives more closely with His will.

CHAPTER 5

TEACH YOUR CHILDREN TO PRAY

Teaching children to pray is one of the most meaningful ways we can help them develop a strong relationship with God. In a world that often feels chaotic, equipping our children with the tools to turn to God in prayer offers them a foundation of faith and a sense of peace that can guide them through all of life's challenges. We combat the rise of a prayerless generation by empowering our children to pray for themselves and intercede for others. Starting early helps to develop a habit and a love for prayer, showing them the importance of consulting God in everything they do.

Raising up the next generation of prayer warriors, intercessors, and watchmen is our responsibility. We are not just raising children; we are preparing the spiritual leaders of tomorrow. We must steward what will come after us, leaving a legacy not just of tangible things but of spiritual depth and devotion—the most valuable inheritance we can offer our children.

One of the best ways to instill this habit is by modeling prayer in front of them. Let them join you in your morning quiet time, prayer, and meditation. Encourage them to pray before meals, when they are nervous, or when they are afraid, teaching them to stop and seek God's guidance in all things. These small, daily practices can have a profound impact on their spiritual growth.

But we can do more than just model prayer; we can actively teach them with simple, child-friendly scriptures that guide their prayers. Here are seven examples:

Child-Friendly Scriptures for Prayer

1. **The Lord's Prayer**
   - "Our Father in heaven, may your name be kept holy. May your Kingdom come soon. May your will be done on earth, as it is in heaven. Give us today the food we need, and forgive us our sins, as we have forgiven those who sin against us. And don't let us yield to temptation, but rescue us from the evil one." *(Matthew 6:9-13, NLT)*
   - This prayer teaches children to pray for God's will, their daily needs, and forgiveness.

2. **Prayer for Protection**
   - "For he will order his angels to protect you wherever you go." *(Psalm 91:11, NLT)*
   - This helps children feel secure, knowing that God's angels watch over them.

3. **Prayer of Thanksgiving**
   - "This is the day the Lord has made. We will rejoice and be glad in it." *(Psalm 118:24, NLT)*

149

- o This prayer encourages children to start their day with gratitude and joy.

4. **Prayer for Help**
   - o "God is our refuge and strength, always ready to help in times of trouble." *(Psalm 46:1, NLT)*
   - o This prayer teaches children to turn to God when they need help or are afraid.

5. **Prayer of Forgiveness**
   - o "But if we confess our sins to him, he is faithful and just to forgive us our sins and to cleanse us from all wickedness." *(1 John 1:9, NLT)*
   - o This prayer helps children understand the importance of seeking forgiveness and knowing that God forgives.

6. **Prayer of Guidance**
   - o "Trust in the Lord with all your heart; do not depend on your own understanding. Seek his will in all you do, and he will show you which path to take." *(Proverbs 3:5-6, NLT)*
   - o This prayer encourages children to trust God and seek His guidance in their decisions.

7. **Prayer of Trust**

   o "But when I am afraid, I will put my trust in you."
      (Psalm 56:3, NLT)

   o This is a simple prayer for children to learn to trust God in scary or uncertain times.

Additional Prayers to Teach your Children

1. **The Lord's Prayer**

   "Dear God, thank you for being our Father in heaven. Help us to do what you want today. Give us what we need, forgive our mistakes, and help us forgive others. Keep us safe from wrong things. Amen."

2. **Prayer for Protection**

   "God, please send your angels to protect me today. Keep me safe wherever I go. Thank you for watching over me. Amen."

3. **Prayer of Thanksgiving**

   "Thank you, God, for this new day! I am so glad you made it. Help me to be happy and grateful today. Amen."

4. **Prayer for Help**

"God, you are my help and strength. When I am in trouble, please help me and make me strong. Thank you for always being there for me. Amen."

5. **Prayer of Forgiveness**

"Dear Jesus, I am sorry for the wrong things I have done. Please forgive me and make my heart clean. Thank you for loving me and forgiving me. Amen."

6. **Prayer for Guidance**

"Lord, help me trust you with all my heart. Show me the right path to take and help me to do what is right. Thank you for guiding me. Amen."

7. **Prayer of Trust**

"God, when I feel scared, I will trust in you. I know you are always with me. Thank you for keeping me safe. Amen."

The need for spiritual training is more urgent than ever. Statistics show that children introduced to prayer at an early age are more likely to maintain their faith in adulthood, yet many parents miss this opportunity. Let us commit to raising a generation that knows the power of prayer.

Begin today by incorporating these practices into your daily routine, teaching your children to pray with scripture, and equipping them to become the prayer warriors, intercessors, and watchmen that the world needs. Together, we can leave a legacy that goes beyond material wealth, one that is rich in faith, spiritual depth, and the love of God.

You need friends that pray! – Shavaunta Harris

"About that time King Herod Agrippa began to persecute some believers in the church. He had the apostle James (John's brother) killed with a sword. When Herod saw how much this pleased the Jewish people, he also arrested Peter. (This took place during the Passover celebration.) Then he imprisoned him, placing him under the guard of four squads of four soldiers each. Herod intended to bring Peter out for public trial after the Passover. But while Peter was in prison, the church prayed very earnestly for him. The night before Peter was to be placed on trial, he was asleep, fastened with two chains between two soldiers. Others stood guard at the prison gate. Suddenly, there was a bright light in the cell, and an angel of the Lord stood before Peter.

The angel struck him on the side to awaken him and said, "Quick! Get up!" And the chains fell off his wrists. Then the angel told him, "Get dressed and put on your sandals." And he did. "Now put on your coat and follow me," the angel ordered. So Peter left the cell, following the angel. But all the time he thought it was a vision. He didn't realize it was actually happening. They passed the first and second guard posts and came to the iron gate leading to the city, and this opened for them all by itself. So they passed through and started walking down the street, and then the angel suddenly left him.

Peter finally came to his senses. "It's really true!" he said. "The Lord has sent his angel and saved me from Herod and from what the Jewish leaders had planned to do to me!" When he realized this, he went to the home of Mary, the mother of John Mark, where many were gathered for prayer. He knocked at the door in the gate, and a servant girl named Rhoda came to open it. When she recognized Peter's voice, she was so overjoyed that, instead of opening the door, she ran back inside and told everyone, "Peter is standing at the door!" "You're out of your mind!" they said. When she insisted, they decided, "It must be his angel." Meanwhile, Peter continued knocking.

When they finally opened the door and saw him, they were amazed. He motioned for them to quiet down and told them how the Lord had led him out of prison. "Tell James and the other brothers what happened," he said. And then he went to another place. At dawn there was a great commotion among the soldiers about what had happened to Peter. Herod Agrippa ordered a thorough search for him. When he couldn't be found, Herod interrogated the guards and sentenced them to death. Afterward Herod left Judea to stay in Caesarea for a while." (Acts 12:1-19, NLT)

This passage of scripture speaks to the power of agreement in prayer. The scripture says while they were imprisoned the church earnestly prayed. While Herod possessed the power to hold the men of God in prison with the authority he possessed in the natural. He was no match for the authority that had been given to his friends in the spiritual. Herod had soldiers and chains, but his friends had access and keys through the power of prayer. Though Peter was bound his friends were not deterred by what they saw. They did not see his situation as hopeless; they knew the power that was in prayer, and they did not hesitate to use it.

I find it funny that nowhere in the scripture does it say Peter prayed for himself, but it was his friends that prayed for his release. Scripture says, Peter was kept in prison, but the church was free to pray. When every other gate is shut and locked, the gate to heaven is wide open. We take advantage of that open gate through prayer. Peter had friends that did not give up on him, talk about him or his situation Peter's friends prayed! Let me say this again...YOU NEED FRIENDS THAT WILL PRAY FOR YOU AND NOT ON YOU! YOU NEED FRIENDS THAT WILL STAND WITH YOU AND WILL PRAY YOU THROUGH.

It is so important to have friends who pray! I cannot even count the number of times I have needed the prayers of a friend—honestly, there have been too many to keep track of. Having friends is great, but having friends who can keep their mouths shut when it comes to gossip but wide open in prayer is a real blessing. I am not only thankful to have praying friends but also to be a praying friend.

I consider myself a watchman for my friends. Growing up, I was the peaceful kid who got along well with everyone. As the oldest of three sisters, I was the calm one, while my middle sister was the complete opposite. She was always ready to fight—just waiting for someone to look at her the wrong way, say the wrong thing, or even give off the appearance of a problem, and she was ready to fight. While I was not like that in the natural world, I am definitely like that in the spirit when it comes to the enemy and spiritual warfare.

I am the friend who will engage in spiritual battle with you, shutting down everything the enemy attempts to do! I go straight to my

Father and PRAY! If somebody is sick, I am going to pray. If you need a miracle, I am going to pray. If you are attacked spiritually, I am going to pray! I believe and have seen the power of prayer.

As Kingdom citizens, we need to understand that we have the incredible ability to counsel with God and petition Him on behalf of others. This is our calling and our power as believers.
Matthew 18:19-20 (ESV) says, **"Again I say to you, if two of you agree on earth about anything they ask, it will be done for them by my Father in heaven. For where two or three are gathered in my name, there am I among them."**

Notice the emphasis on the plural—**two** or **three**. There is undeniable power in agreement and in praying with friends, praying for and with each other. If we look at the Lord's Prayer, it is not a singular prayer but a plural one: "Our Father in heaven, hallowed be your name..." This highlights the power of unity and collective prayer. There's immense strength in coming together in agreement, lifting up each other's burdens, and seeking God's intervention as a unified body. So, let us embrace the power of praying together, knowing that where two or three are gathered in His name, He is right there with us.

Testimonies of The Power of Prayer

The Bible speaks of believers overcoming through the power of their testimonies. I would like to share a few testimonies that reveal the incredible power of prayer in my life and in the life of one of my sisters in Christ. I asked my friend to share a time when she struggled in her walk with the Lord, specifically in prayer. This is her testimony, which I believe will encourage and challenge us all to persevere through difficult seasons and look to the Lord, our true source of hope. After reading her testimony, you will find two of my personal testimonies, which I believe will continue to inspire and encourage you to grow in prayer and deeper communion with God.

Weary in my Faith Testimony

I recall a time when I struggled to get a prayer through; it was because my faith had grown weary. Mark 9:23-24, Jesus tells a desperate father, "'If you can?' said Jesus. 'Everything is possible for one who believes.' Immediately the boy's father exclaimed, 'I do believe; help me overcome my unbelief!'" You may wonder: Is it possible to believe and still struggle with unbelief?

Yes, absolutely. In this passage, a father watched the torment of his son by a spirit since childhood. He approached Jesus and called Him "teacher," saying, "I brought you my son who has a mute spirit." Here are three things that stood out to me in this scripture:

The father called Jesus "teacher."

He brought his son to the disciples to cast out the spirit, but they could not.

This situation had been going on for years, and none of his efforts to fix it had worked.

The father believed in Jesus, but he still needed help with his unbelief. He knew Jesus as "teacher" but, after seeing His disciples fail, was unsure what would happen. Yet, he was desperate—just like I was during a time in my life. I remember when I, too, believed, but I needed God to help my faith for the situation I was facing. As a single mother of seven children, with no support from their fathers, I was working multiple jobs—cleaning, making gift baskets, painting, and sewing clothes—just to make ends meet. Despite all my hard work, it was never enough. I fell behind on rent, and the landlord filed for eviction. I received a three-day notice, then a 30-day notice to vacate.

I was angry, depleted, and frustrated. I did not pray because, in my mind, God had seen how hard I was working, and it still was not enough. I accepted the situation, believing, "This is my life, and it will not change." My faith was weary, and I did not open my mouth to tell God how hurt, tired, and frustrated I was.

At that point in my walk with Christ, I only knew God as the Creator of the universe, the one who gave His Son to save us. But I did not know how to truly lean in on those truths in my daily struggles. As eviction day approached, with no money, nowhere to go, and nothing packed, I finally prayed, "God, help us, please! I have worked hard, and You said You do not want anyone to perish. Where are You? We need You now!"

After that transparent, desperate prayer, I told my children to start packing. They asked, "Where are we going?" I responded, "I do not know, but God has to provide." While getting boxes, I spoke to someone on the phone and said, "God is going to send someone to give us the keys to a house!" I was desperate for a miracle.

The next morning, around 7 AM, the doorbell rang. It was my neighbor from across the street, who I only knew in passing. She asked, "Do you need a place to live?" I was shocked. I said, "Excuse me." She then explained that she and her husband had decided to move to the country the night before, and they wanted to offer me their house rent-free for three months, all the utilities were on, and I could paint the house any color I wanted.

She handed me the keys and said, "We will be gone in a week." I lost it! I begin to cry, thanking her and thanking God! I wanted to take off and run around the block in my PJ's. I was so overwhelmed with gratitude! The house was identical to the one where we lived in—no U-Haul needed and there was no disruption to my children's schooling. When it was time to move I was putting couches on kids backs (lol). God provided just what we needed.

Yes, I believed, but I needed God to help my unbelief, and He did. He heard my desperate prayer and answered in a way only He could. Prayer is our lifeline—it is how we communicate with the One who can fix every situation. Even when our faith is weak or when doubt creeps in, we must go to God in honesty and brokenness. That is when His ear is most open to hear us. He is Jehovah Jireh—our provider."

~Amelia Mosley

Prayer Never Expires

One of the most profound experiences I hold dear is when I prayed for my brother-in-law as he battled addiction. It was a heartbreaking time for my husband, who was deeply burdened by his brother's struggle. One evening, after finishing a prayer call, just as I was about to go to bed, I felt the Holy Spirit nudging me to pray specifically for him.

During that prayer, I asked God to make my brother-in-law uncomfortable in the situations where he had once found solace. I prayed that he would grow weary of the lifestyle he was trapped in. Just two days later, as my husband and I were preparing for bed, we received an unexpected call. My brother-in-law was on his way over to our house. When he arrived, he said something that took my breath away—he told us he just could not get comfortable and felt compelled to leave where he was. His words mirrored the very prayer I had lifted up to God. In that moment, I rejoiced in the goodness and faithfulness of God, knowing that the power of prayer had brought my brother-in-law back home.

Though he faced more struggles and relapses after that night, one thing remains clear: prayer never expires. It is an ongoing conversation with God, and no matter what situation you or your loved ones are going through, never stop praying. Hold on to the prayers you have lifted up, trusting that God will answer in His perfect timing. Today, my brother-in-law has been sober and clean for two years, and now works in a facility helping others overcome addiction.

Pew Research Center Study

Prayer is not just a spiritual exercise; it is a powerful tool that can change lives. Studies have shown that people who pray regularly experience lower levels of stress, increased feelings of hope, and a greater sense of peace. In a survey conducted by the Pew Research Center, 68% of Americans reported that they pray every day. Yet, how many of us truly understand the impact our prayers can have on the lives of others?

What if you were the person God wanted to use to bring your loved one out of addiction? Or to help someone you care about develop the strength to leave an abusive relationship? My brother-in-law did not know I was praying for him, but I knew that if I came before God on his behalf, the Lord would respond. I am not claiming that my prayers were the only factor in his deliverance, but I know that God allowed me to play a role, and that role was through prayer.

So, I want to encourage you—yes you, as you read this right now—to take on the responsibility of interceding for those God has placed on your heart.

Carry the burden of lifting up those who need His intervention. Be the one who stands in the gap, who prays without ceasing, and who believes in the power of prayer to bring about transformation.

This is your call to action: Do not just read these testimonies and move on. Let them inspire you to pray more fervently, to intercede more passionately, and to trust that God is listening. Whether you are praying for a loved one struggling with addiction, a friend facing a difficult diagnosis, or even for your own challenges—know that your prayers matter. They have the power to change lives, to bring hope, and to invite God's miraculous intervention into the most desperate situations.

Accept the mantle of prayer today. Be the person who prays, who believes, and who trusts that God can and will move in the lives of those you care about. Your prayers can be effective, just as they did for my brother-in-law. Let us continue to seek God's face, intercede for others, and witness the power of prayer unfold in our lives and in the lives of those we love.

Weary in Prayer – My Testimony

I was introduced to prayer in 2013 during a really rough time in my life. I had a close friend who always invited me to church, but I just did not have any desire to go. Reflecting back on that time, I cannot stress enough how important it is to be persistent with the people you are praying for and those you have a connection with. Today, I walk with the Lord because a friend was persistent in bringing me to the Lord. Keep inviting them, and do not give up praying for them.

I remember a season when God assigned me to lead a prayer call twice a day every Monday, Wednesday, and Friday. This was part of my women's mentoring ministry, and I committed myself to host these calls and lead the women God brought into my life in persistent prayer. One morning, while leading the call, I felt incredibly discouraged and after praying for all the requests of those on the call I had nothing left to pray for my own problems. After the call ended, two of my close friends reached out to me. Even though I did not say anything on the call, one of my friends sensed gravity, heaviness and discouragement and drove right over to my house to pray for me. God knew that I needed to be refreshed and washed in prayer so that my spirit man could continue to endure.

There will be times when you will not have the strength to pray. In those moments, lean on those God has placed in your life to pray for you. You need friends who pray! The Bible shows us the power of collective prayer and unity. In Acts 2, the believers were together in agreement, and the Holy Spirit fell upon them because they were willing to pray together. Even Jesus needed His friends to pray with Him in the Garden of Gethsemane.

Prayer is a spiritual discipline that every believer should practice and develop personally. However, there are seasons in our lives where we need people who will pray with us and help us push through in prayer. The Bible tells us that one can put a thousand to flight, but two can put ten thousand to flight. The power of agreement and unity in prayer can break things in the spiritual realm.

Think about the Lord's Prayer. It starts with "Our Father," not "My Father," emphasizing the collective nature of prayer. If you do not have a prayer partner, seek out someone whose life has evidence of a consistent prayer life and ask them to be your prayer partner. Unified prayer is a gift God has given to assist with growth in our prayer life.

When I first got saved and started my journey in prayer I was determined to build my relationship with God. I learned that the two most effective ways to do so was through reading my Bible and praying. The church I was attending at the time had prayer built in the foundation of everything. This was a wonderful way for me to begin to feed the hunger I had to grow in prayer. I began attending my church's prayer meetings, joined the prayer team, and connected with the prayer leader. Building these relationships took time and were important to my growth in prayer.

Prayer is not a race; it is a journey. Seek out those God has appointed to your life and pray about the people already connected to you. I remember being drawn to the ministry of prayer, watching people get delivered and set free. I knew prayer was in me, but I had no idea how to express it until I connected with my church's prayer leader.

I remember my first time leading a prayer call. I was nervous and full of doubts, but I pressed on, reciting scriptures like Psalm 34:4 "I prayed to the Lord, and he answered me. He freed me from all my fears." until I had the courage to dial in. Once I did, something ignited in me. My relationship with God grew, and so did my confidence in prayer.

People began to share how my prayers had blessed them, how they got jobs, were healed, or experienced financial breakthroughs. I never knew this power was in me until I stepped out and connected with other prayer warriors. Now, I lead, and host prayer calls at my church, set the atmosphere before service, lead a mentoring group in prayer, and encourage other women to cultivate a relationship of prayer with God. None of this would have happened if I had not stepped out in faith and connected with other believers.

You need friends who pray. Seek out those who can help you grow in prayer. If Jesus needed friends to pray with Him, we must find people to help us grow in our prayer life. It will not be easy, and the enemy will try to convince you that you can do it alone, but that is far from the truth. There is power in unity and praying with others. When you face great trials, you will need the prayers of friends who can support you when you cannot pray for yourself.

Prayer Accountability Partner Assignment

Prayer accountability partner: As we conclude this chapter, I want to present you with a prayer assignment. We have discussed the importance of having friends who pray. I want you to pray about connecting with some prayer accountability partners. It may be your neighbor, coworker, family member, or someone at your church, Bible study, or youth group.

Find one to two people you can pray with regularly. Building a consistent and fervent prayer life is the focus of an accountability partner. Ask God specifically to show you who to connect with to help you grow in prayer, in partnership with the Holy Spirit. It could be the worship leader, someone on the welcome team, or even someone you least expect. Step out of your comfort zone and walk in faith. Write down two people you have come in contact with who will help you grow in prayer this year.

1. _____

2. _____

After you have identified your prayer partners, begin to pray for them, pray for them as you pray for yourself, pray for their families, pray for their health, pray for their relationships, and even for your connection with them. Keep in mind, I am not saying that you can only have two people helping you with prayer.

I just wanted to give you a starting point. However they will change, there will be many people that will come across your path to help you grow in prayer. Be open to what God says and obedient to His voice and walk the journey but most of all enjoy it. Look forward to the remarkable things God will reveal in your prayer time.

CHAPTER 6

POSTURES OF PRAYER

What is a prayer posture?

The dictionary's definition of posture is the attitude or the position of the body when it is stationary or moving. This is correct for the natural, however the natural posture has spiritual implications. When I speak of spiritual posture I am speaking of your heart posture specifically when in prayer. Your posture in the spirit expresses the attitudes of your heart. A posture in prayer speaks to God about your desire for Him and what you need.

In this chapter, we will be exploring the different postures of prayer in the physical and the spiritual and their meaning. Posture is important in hearing God. God is not so much concerned with our physical posture as He is with our spiritual posture.

1. **Adoration** - is reverence, respect, admiration, and devotion. The Latin word for adoration is *adoratio*, meaning to give homage to someone or something. This may be expressed through our words, actions, or both. Simply put, It is expressing love, reverence, and awe for God.

Scripture examples of adoration:

o "Praise the Lord, my soul; all my innermost being, praise his holy name. Praise the Lord, my soul, and forget not all his benefits—who forgives all your sins and heals all your diseases, who redeems your life from the pit and crowns you with love and compassion, who satisfies your desires with good things so that your youth is renewed like the eagle's." *(Psalms 103:1-5)*

o "Oh come, let us worship and bow down; let us kneel before the Lord, our Maker!" *(Psalms 95:6)*

o "Exalt the Lord our God; worship at his footstool! Holy is he!" *(Psalm 99:5)*

o "Worthy are you, our Lord and God, to receive glory and honor and power, for you created all things, and by your will they existed and were created." *(Revelation 4:11)*

o "Who will not fear, O Lord, and glorify your name? For you alone are holy. All nations will come and worship you, for your righteous acts have been revealed." *(Revelation 15:4)*

2. **Exhort(ation)** - to urge strongly, encourage, egg-on, press upon, goad, or prompt. The word in Latin is *hortari*, meaning "to incite," and it often implies urging or admonishing. Exhortation can be impressing upon others or strongly encourage or advise earnestly in corporate or private prayer.

Scripture examples of adoration:

o "The Lord is my strength and my song, and he has become my salvation; this is my God, and I will praise him, my father's God, and I will exalt him." *(Exodus 15:2)*

o "Finally, be strong in the Lord and in the strength of his might." *(Ephesians 6:10)*

o "For the Lord your God is he who goes with you to fight for you against your enemies, to give you the victory." *(Deuteronomy 20:4)*

o "Have I not commanded you? Be strong and courageous. Do not be frightened, and do not be dismayed, for the Lord your God is with you wherever you go." *(Joshua 1:9)* o "Behold, God is my salvation; I will trust, and will not be afraid; for the Lord God is my strength and my song, and he has become my salvation." *(Isaiah 12:2)*

o "He gives power to the faint, and to him who has no might he increases strength." *(Isaiah 40:29)*

o "Be strong, and let your heart take courage, all you who wait for the Lord!" *(Psalms 31:24)*

3. **Submission**: to come under the authority of God and yield, surrender to His will. It is a place of humility and obedience unto God. (1 Peter 2:13)

4. **Supplication: bowing or kneeling in submission.**
   (1 Kings 8:34)
   o **Supplication can also be associated with** asking and seeking God earnestly, making a plea or cry out to God.
      o 1 Kings 8:28
      o 2 Chronicles 6:19
      o Psalm 28:2; 30:8; 31:22; 142:1
      o Hebrews 5:7
      o Especially, consider Psalm 142:1, which states, "I cried unto the LORD with my voice; with my voice unto the LORD did I make my supplication."

174

The word is also used with the idea of weeping in three passages (Jeremiah 3:21; 31:9; Hosea 12:4). Supplication is an attitude or spirit of prayer. We submit to His will and authority. We earnestly seek His help. In this way, we make supplication to our God in our prayers (Hebrews 5:7)

5. **Confession: confession is God's mechanism to restore a broken relationship between Him and us hence why confession can be prayers that acknowledge our sin. The kind of prayer confession we are speaking of for the purpose of this book is** admitting or acknowledging something that is already true. In prayer confession you are taking God's Word of truth and confessing it from your mouth in prayer. Seeking God's Word in prayer confession give strategy and target prayers that will move the heart of God because He responds to His word. Here are some examples of prayer confessions.

Daniels prayer confession:

"I prayed to the Lord my God and confessed: Lord, the great and awesome God, who keeps his covenant of love with those who love him and keep his commandments, we have sinned and done wrong. We have been wicked and have rebelled; we have turned away from your commands and laws. We have not listened to your servants the prophets, who spoke in your name to our kings, our princes and our ancestors,

and to all the people of the land. The Lord our God is merciful and forgiving, even though we have rebelled against him; we have not obeyed the Lord our God or kept the laws he gave us through his servants the prophets." (Daniel 9:4-6;9-10)

Nehemiah's prayer confession:

"Lord, the God of heaven, the great and awesome God, who keeps his covenant of love with those who love him and keep his commandments, let your ear be attentive and your eyes open to hear the prayer your servant is praying before you day and night for your servants, the people of Israel. I confess the sins we Israelites, including myself and my father's family, have committed against you. We have acted very wickedly toward you. We have not obeyed the commands, decrees and laws you gave your servant Moses." (Nehemiah 1:5-7)

David's prayer of confession after his affair with Bathsheba:

Have mercy on me, O God, because of your unfailing love. Because of your great compassion, blot out the stain of my sins. Wash me clean from my guilt. Purify me from my sin. For I recognize my rebellion; it haunts me day and night. Against you, and you alone, have I sinned; I have done what is evil in your sight. You will be proved right in what you say, and your judgment against me is just. (Psalms 51:1-4)

Each of these three biblical confessions include a humble heart, acknowledgement of a specific sin, affirmation of God's character and assurance of forgiveness. These same elements should be present in our prayer confessions as well.

Physical posture representing these positions are honoring God

Spiritual posture is our approach to prayer as we speak to God. Communication with God does not require physical position but each posture gives expression to the attitude of our heart.

- o **Standing:** giving honor like standing in a courtroom or for a dignitary, this is a type of celebratory prayer and thanksgiving. We think of a standing ovation. (Psalms 65:8)

- o **Sitting in prayer:** Sitting in prayer can symbolize a posture of stillness, humility, and attentiveness before God. It represents taking time to be in God's presence, listening for His voice, and opening one's heart to communication with Him. Unlike other postures such as kneeling or standing, sitting in prayer often conveys a sense of resting in God's presence, trusting in His care, and reflecting on His guidance. It can also signify a personal, intimate conversation with God, where one seeks to deepen their relationship and surrender their burdens.
  (Luke 10:39, Matthew 11:28-29)

- o **Kneeling:** is a sign of surrender, humility, and recognition. Kneeling means to bring yourself low. Daniel kneeled frequently in prayer.
  - o Daniel 6:10
  - o Matthew 17:14
  - o Mark 1:40
  - o Mark 10:17
  - o Romans 14:11

- o **Bowing**: (adoration and honor reverence in bowing) having a brought yourself low worshiping and giving God your attention. (1 Kings 18:42 and 2 Chronicles 7:3)

- o **Lifting**: our eyes to heaven (*focused intentionally on what is in front of you*).
  - o John 17
  - o Psalms 121:1-2
  - o Psalms 123:1
  - o Daniel 4:34
  - o John 11:41

- ○ **Lying prostrate/on your face in prayer:** a sign of humility and submission, respect to honor someone.
  - ○ Genesis 17:3
  - ○ Genesis 4:26
  - ○ Exodus 33:10
  - ○ Leviticus 9:24
  - ○ Deuteronomy 26:10
  - ○ 2 chronicles 29:29

- ○ **Raising hands**: Praise and Honor and worship.
  - ○ 1 Kings 8:42
  - ○ Psalms 28:1-2

Building your endurance in prayer

Endurance, often referred to in scripture as perseverance or steadfastness, is a critical aspect of a powerful prayer life. To build endurance in prayer means to persist in seeking God even when circumstances are difficult, answers seem delayed, or the path ahead is unclear. The Bible emphasizes the importance of this perseverance, encouraging believers not to grow weary but to continue faithfully in their prayer lives.

One key scripture that highlights the necessity of endurance is James 1:2-4 "Consider it pure joy, my brothers, and sisters, whenever you face trials of many kinds, because you know that the testing of your faith produces perseverance. Let perseverance finish its work so that you may be mature and complete, not lacking anything."

This passage highlights the truth that trials and delays are often opportunities for spiritual growth. In prayer, it is through persistently seeking God's will, that we are shaped and matured. Endurance in prayer is not just about getting answers; it is about allowing the process to refine and grow us into deeper intimacy with God.

Building Endurance in Prayer When Answers Are Delayed – Practical Examples

When we pray and do not immediately see results, it is easy to become discouraged. But scripture reminds us that waiting is part of God's plan. Romans 12:12 encourages us to "be joyful in hope, patient in affliction, and faithful in prayer."

For example, if you have been praying for the salvation of a loved one for years without seeing change, the call is to persist. Though the answer has not come within the time limit you hoped for, your endurance is a testament of faith. Continue praying, believing that God is working in ways you cannot yet see.

Pushing Through Weariness

In Galatians 6:9, Paul writes, "Let us not become weary in doing good, for at the proper time we will reap a harvest if we do not give up." This principle applies to prayer just as much as it does to any other act of faith. There will be times when prayer feels like a burden, when it is tempting to give up because of exhaustion or spiritual fatigue. But God calls us to push through, trusting that there is a harvest of blessing, growth, or answered prayers on the other side of our persistence.

For instance, consider a mother praying daily for her children's protection and spiritual growth. Though the day-to-day grind of life may make it hard to stay focused, her persistent prayers will have lasting effects. The unseen work of God often takes time to bear visible fruit, but she continues, knowing that her prayers are part of a divine process.

Endurance in Prayer Through Trials

Trials can make it difficult to maintain a consistent prayer life, but they are also opportunities to deepen our endurance. Romans 5:3-4 teaches us, "Not only that, but we rejoice in our sufferings, knowing that suffering produces endurance, and endurance produces character, and character produces hope." When we face challenges—whether health crises, financial struggles, or relational difficulties—our prayers become the vehicle through which God builds resilience and character within us.

Imagine someone battling a chronic illness. Their prayers for healing may not be answered immediately, but as they endure through the pain and continue to seek God's presence, they discover a deeper level of faith. This endurance strengthens their spirit, allowing them to rely on God's grace and hope more than ever before.

Persistent Prayer: Jesus' Example

The ultimate example of endurance in prayer is found in Jesus Himself. In Luke 22:42-44, we see Jesus in the Garden of Gethsemane, praying before His crucifixion: "Father, if you are willing, take this cup from me; yet not my will, but yours be done. An angel from heaven appeared to him and strengthened him. And being in anguish, he prayed more earnestly, and his sweat was like drops of blood falling to the ground."

Even in the face of overwhelming agony, Jesus continued to pray, surrendering His will to the Father. His endurance in prayer, despite knowing the suffering ahead, shows us that persistence is often accompanied by deep emotional and spiritual struggle. But in that struggle, God provides the strength we need to continue.

Endurance Brings Maturity

Building endurance in prayer is not about just "hanging on" until we get what we want. It is about transforming our hearts and minds to align with God's will. Through persistent prayer, we develop the spiritual muscles needed to withstand life's trials, and we grow closer to God in the process. As we learn to pray without ceasing, as Paul urges in 1 Thessalonians 5:17, we open ourselves to God's timing, trusting that He hears us and is at work—even when we do not see immediate results. Endurance in prayer is a journey, and each moment of persistence brings us into greater maturity and intimacy with the Lord.

"But you, dear friends, must build each other up in your most holy faith, pray in the power of the Holy Spirit, and await the mercy of our Lord Jesus Christ, who will bring you eternal life. In this way, you will keep yourselves safe in God's love." *(Jude 1: 20-21)*

As you grow and mature in prayer you will need to continue to be built up in the spirit. We should be deepening our relationship with God through the Holy spirit. Being edified and empowered to stand in the place of prayer through every season by prayer and the help of the Holy spirit.

Prayers of Thanksgiving

Prayers of thanksgiving are foundational in the Christian faith, as they express gratitude and acknowledgment of God's goodness, provision, and faithfulness. Here is a detailed practical explanation of prayers of thanksgiving:

1. Reflect on God's Blessings: Begin by reflecting on the blessings in your life. Consider your family, friends, health, provisions, opportunities, and any other blessings you have received. Take time to recognize and appreciate the abundance of God's goodness in your life.

2. Create a Thankful Atmosphere: Find a quiet and comfortable place where you can pray without distractions. Set the mood for thanksgiving by playing worship music, reading relevant Bible verses, or simply quieting your heart and mind to focus on God's presence.

3. Express Gratitude: Approach God with a heart full of gratitude. Begin your prayer by addressing God and expressing your thankfulness for specific blessings. Be sincere and heartfelt in your expression of gratitude, acknowledging His goodness and faithfulness in your life.

4. Be Specific: Offer specific thanksgiving for the blessings you have received. Instead of generic statements, mention particular instances or gifts for which you are thankful. This specificity demonstrates attentiveness to God's work in your life and fosters a deeper connection with Him.

5. Use Scripture: Incorporate relevant Bible verses into your prayer of thanksgiving. Scripture is rich with passages that emphasize thanksgiving and praise. You can personalize these verses and use them as expressions of gratitude to God.

6. Reflect on God's Character: Take time to reflect on God's character and attributes as you pray. Thank Him for whom He is—loving, merciful, gracious, compassionate, and faithful. Acknowledge His sovereignty over your life and His steadfast presence in every circumstance.

7. Express Thankfulness for Spiritual Blessings: Do not forget to thank God for spiritual blessings such as salvation, forgiveness of sins, the gift of His Son Jesus Christ, the indwelling of the Holy Spirit, and the hope of eternal life. These blessings are foundational to your faith and worthy of continual thanksgiving.

8. Commit to Thankfulness: Close your prayer by committing to live a life of thankfulness. Ask God to help you cultivate a heart of gratitude in all circumstances, whether in times of abundance or adversity. Express your desire to glorify God through a lifestyle of gratitude and praise.

9. End with Praise: Conclude your prayer with words of praise and adoration. Lift up God's name and magnify His greatness, declaring His worthiness of all honor, glory, and praise.

10. Continue in Thanksgiving: Finally, remember that prayers of thanksgiving are not limited to specific times or occasions. Cultivate a habit of thanksgiving by incorporating it into your daily prayer life. Regularly pause to thank God throughout your day, recognizing His presence and blessings in every moment.

By following these practical steps, you can engage in heartfelt prayers of thanksgiving that deepen your relationship with God and cultivate a spirit of gratitude in your life.

A biblical prayer of thanksgiving is a prayer that expresses gratitude and thankfulness to God for His blessings, provisions, and faithfulness. Here is an example of a biblical prayer of thanksgiving:

o   *"Lord, I thank you for your abundant blessings in my life. You are the source of all good things, and I am grateful for your provision and care. Thank you for the gift of life, for my health, for my family and friends, and for the many ways you have shown your love to me. Thank you for your forgiveness and grace, for guiding me through difficult times, and for always being faithful, even when I am not. Help me to live each day with a heart full of gratitude and to honor you with all that I am. In Jesus' name, Amen."*

This prayer reflects the biblical principles of acknowledging God's goodness, expressing gratitude for His blessings, and committing to live in thankfulness each day.

Praying Amiss

"Praying amiss" refers to praying with the wrong motives, intentions, or in a way that is outside of God's will. It occurs when our prayers are driven by selfish desires, personal gain, or are disconnected from the purposes of God.

The Bible addresses this in James 4:3 (NLT), which says, "And even when you ask, you don't get it because your motives are all wrong—you want only what will give you pleasure." This scripture shows that when we pray solely for our own desires, without considering God's will or the needs of others, our prayers are ineffective.

Additionally, 1 John 5:14 (NLT) reminds us of the importance of praying in line with God's will: "And we are confident that he hears us whenever we ask for anything that pleases him."

Prayers aligned with God's will are heard and answered, while prayers that are self-centered or misaligned with His purpose are not. Therefore, to avoid praying amiss, believers must seek to understand God's heart, align their desires with His, and pray with the intention of fulfilling His greater plans for their lives.

Prayers that are selfish, self-centered, out of alignment with God's will, or prayed with the wrong motives and heart, will not be prioritized by God. He is not obligated to answer prayers that contradict His divine purpose for your life. Let me be clear—this is not a book that will encourage you to keep praying if you are out of the Father's will.

When your life is not in line with God's plan, you cannot expect Him to move on your behalf. As it says in James 4:3, "And even when you ask, you don't get it because your motives are all wrong—you want only what will give you pleasure."

Examples of Praying Amiss

Praying for Material Wealth Out of Greed

o Asking God for excessive wealth or possessions purely out of greed or a desire to impress others.

Praying for Personal Revenge

o Asking God to harm or punish someone out of personal vendetta or bitterness rather than seeking reconciliation and forgiveness.

Praying for Success to Boost Ego

o Seeking success, recognition, or promotion primarily to boost one's ego or gain power over others, rather than using it to serve and honor God.

Silent prayers get God's attention too!

Silent prayers get God's attention too! There are times when words fail us, and in those moments, God steps in with His power to help us pray. We've all experienced times when we had no words to express the depth of our feelings, pain, or confusion. I remember a season in my own walk with God, when I was growing in prayer, but I simply had no words. In those moments, I discovered the power of wordless prayers—times when I could not even bring myself to speak. Yet, the Holy Spirit was present, understanding my heart when I had no words.

Romans 8:26 reassures us: "In the same way, the Spirit helps us in our weakness. We do not know what we ought to pray for, but the Spirit himself intercedes for us through wordless groans." The Holy Spirit can understand and interpret the prayers we carry in our hearts, even when we cannot express them. We do not always have to tell God through spoken words what is on our hearts or what is happening in our lives.

Some of the most powerful prayers may be the ones formed in the midst of silent tears, unspoken anguish, or quiet moments of reflection. These are the prayers whispered in the stillness of a bathroom, the car ride home, or in the early hours of the morning.

David understood this intimacy with God when he wrote, "Even before a word is on my tongue, behold, O Lord, you know it altogether." *(Psalm 139:4)*

God is not like us; He does not need words to understand us. He hears what is unspoken because He listens to the heart. As 1 Samuel 16:7 says, "Man looks at the outward appearance, but the Lord looks at the heart." When we do not have the strength to speak, God hears the groaning of our spirits, and that is just as meaningful as any spoken prayer.

It is okay to go into prayer and sit in silence. Often, we feel we need to fill the space with words, but sometimes, the most profound moments in prayer come when we allow ourselves to simply be still. Silent prayers allow space for God to speak, and listening is a vital part of communication with Him. Do not feel pressured to always have the "right" words. Sit in His presence, and trust that He hears the cry of your heart, even when it is unspoken.

Listening Prayers

Listening is an especially important part of prayer as well. Listening prayer is a form of prayer where we pause to hear God's voice instead of doing all the talking. It is an intimate conversation with God where we seek His guidance, wisdom, and reassurance, often allowing

Him to speak into our hearts and lives. While traditional prayer involves us bringing our requests and thoughts to God, listening prayer requires us to quiet our minds, focus on God's presence, and be open to receiving His direction.

Why is Listening Prayer Important?

Listening prayer is vital because it shifts the focus from our needs and concerns to God's voice and will. It deepens our relationship with God and helps us to align our lives with His purposes. This type of prayer is not just about speaking but also about tuning into the still, small voice of the Holy Spirit, who guides us in truth and wisdom.

Biblical Foundations for Listening Prayer

The Bible is full of examples where God's people sought to hear His voice and received guidance, comfort, and direction as a result.

1. **Samuel's Listening Heart**
    o   Scripture:1 Samuel 3:9-10 (NLT)
    o   Story: When the young Samuel was in the temple, God called out to him. Initially, Samuel did not recognize God's voice, but with the guidance of Eli, he responded, "Speak, Lord, your servant is listening." This story illustrates the importance of being open and receptive to God's voice, even when we may not recognize it at first.

2. **Elijah and the Still Small Voice**
    o   Scripture: 1 Kings 19:11-13 (NLT)
    o   Story: The prophet Elijah expected to hear God in the powerful wind, earthquake, and fire, but God spoke to him in a gentle whisper. This teaches us that God often speaks to us in quiet, subtle ways, and we need to be attentive to hear Him.

3. **Jesus' Example of Seeking God's Will**

   o Scripture: Luke 6:12-13 (NLT)

   o Story: Before choosing His twelve disciples, Jesus spent an entire night in prayer. This demonstrates the importance of seeking God's guidance before making significant decisions. Jesus' time in prayer was not just about asking for help but about listening and aligning His actions with the Father's will.

How to Practice Listening Prayer

1. Find a Quiet Space: Set aside time in a place free from distractions where you can focus on God. Silence your phone, close the door, and allow yourself to be still.

2. Start with Scripture: Begin your time by reading a passage of scripture. This helps to focus your mind on God's Word and can serve as a springboard for what He may want to say to you.

3. Invite God to Speak: Ask God to speak to you and make your heart and mind receptive to His voice. You might say something like, "Lord, I am here to listen. Please speak to me and guide my thoughts."

4. **Be Still and Listen:** Quiet your mind and wait. This might make you feel uncomfortable at first, especially if you are used to filling the silence with words. But give God space to speak. He might bring a thought, a scripture, a sense of peace, or a prompting to your heart.

5. **Journal What You Hear:** Writing down what you sense God is saying can help clarify His voice. Reflect on these thoughts later and see how they align with scripture and your circumstances.

6. **Test What You Hear:** It is important to test what you believe you heard from God. Compare it with scripture, and seek counsel from mature Christians if needed. God's voice will never contradict His word.

Personal Experience:

In my own life, practicing listening prayer has transformed my relationship with God. I remember a season when I felt lost and unsure about my next steps. In those moments, instead of bombarding God with requests, I sat in silence, simply asking Him to speak. Over time, I began to feel His guidance in ways I had not before—a sense of peace about certain decisions and clear direction for others. Listening prayer has become a vital part of my spiritual life, helping me to navigate life's challenges with God's wisdom.

Call to action

If you've never tried listening to God during prayer, I encourage you to start today. Begin with just a few minutes each day, inviting God to speak into your life. The more you practice, the more you will recognize His voice and feel His guidance. According to a survey by the Barna Group, while 79% of American Christians say prayer is important, only a small percentage regularly engage in listening prayer. Let us change the statistics. Make listening prayer a regular part of your spiritual routine and see how it deepens your walk with God.

Listening prayer is not just a practice; it is a lifestyle of tuning into God's voice and letting Him lead you. Start today, and experience the difference it makes in your life.

The Cries of Prayer

Your tears get Gods attention. The word cry in many passages of scripture can be interchanged for the word prayer. For instance, there were many times where the children of Israel cried out to the Lord and scripture says, and the Lord answered. Your cry to the Father in prayer is one that gets His attention. The Lord responds to the cries of His children.

Here are some examples of when the children of Israel cried out, even after their sin, the Lord responded:

Consistent Cry Exodus 2:22

Exodus 2:22, NLT states: "Later she gave birth to a son, and Moses named him Gershom, for he explained, 'I have been a foreigner in a foreign land.'" While this verse itself does not directly speak about prayer, it is part of a larger context where consistent prayer is implied and reflected in the life of Moses and the Israelites. The context surrounding this verse shows how the Israelites cried out to God during their oppression in Egypt.

In the broader narrative (Exodus 2:23-25), it is revealed that the Israelites' consistent prayers and cries for deliverance were heard by God. The passage describes how the Israelites groaned in their slavery and cried out, and their cry for help because of their slavery went up to God. This shows a consistent pattern of calling upon God in their distress, demonstrating persistent prayer.

God's response to their prayers is significant, as it leads to the calling of Moses to deliver the Israelites from Egypt. This illustrates the power of consistent prayer in bringing about divine intervention. Therefore, while Exodus 2:22 does not explicitly mention prayer, it is part of a larger narrative that highlights the importance of consistent prayer, as seen in the Israelites' desperate cries to God and His subsequent deliverance.

Persistent Cry: The widow going to the unjust judge

Luke 18:1-8 , NLT: An example of persistent prayer is in the parable of the persistent widow in Luke 18:1-8. In this parable, Jesus tells the story of a widow who repeatedly comes to a judge, seeking justice against her adversary. The judge, who neither fears God nor respects people, initially refuses to help her. However, because the widow is persistent, the judge eventually grants her request.

Here is the passage from Luke 18:1-8:

"One day Jesus told his disciples a story to show that they should always pray and never give up. "There was a judge in a certain city," he said, "who neither feared God nor cared about people. A widow of that city came to him repeatedly, saying, 'Give me justice in this dispute with my enemy.' The judge ignored her for a while, but finally he said to himself, 'I don't fear God or care about people, but this woman is driving me crazy. I'm going to see that she gets justice because she is wearing me out with her constant requests!'"

Then the Lord said, "Learn a lesson from this unjust judge. Even he rendered a just decision in the end. So don't you think God will surely give justice to his chosen people who cry out to him day and night? Will he keep putting them off? I tell you, he will grant justice to them quickly! But when the Son of Man returns, how many will he find on the earth who have faith?"

This parable illustrates the importance of persistent prayer and faith. Jesus uses the widow's persistence as an example to encourage believers to continue praying and not give up, even when the answers are delayed. The unjust judge eventually responds to the widow's persistence, and Jesus contrasts this with God's character, emphasizing that if an unjust judge can be moved by persistence, how much more will a just and loving God respond to the persistent prayers of His people.

This story encourages us to remain steadfast in prayer, trusting that God hears our cries and will respond according to His perfect timing and will.

Misunderstood cry: Hanna and Eli - 1 Samuel 1:15

Hannah deeply distressed because she was unable to have children, desperately prayed to God, pouring out her heart in silent prayer. Her lips moved, but no one could hear her. Eli, the high priest, saw her and mistakenly thought she was drunk.

o *"Oh no, sir!"* she replied. *"I haven't been drinking wine or anything stronger. But I am very discouraged, and I was pouring out my heart to the Lord. Don't think I am a wicked woman! For I have been praying out of great anguish and sorrow."*

Eli misunderstood Hannah's silent and intense prayer as the actions of someone who was intoxicated. However, when Hannah explained her situation, Eli realized his mistake and blessed her, asking God to grant her request. This encounter highlights how deep, personal cries to God can sometimes be misunderstood by others who are not aware of the internal struggles and pain behind those prayers.

Hannah's story encourages believers to persist in prayer, even when others might not understand their distress or the depth of their need. It also serves as a reminder not to judge others based on appearances, as there may be unseen reasons for their actions.

Desperate cry: Bartimaeus

As Jesus was leaving Jericho with His disciples and a large crowd, Bartimaeus, a blind beggar, was sitting by the roadside. When he heard that it was Jesus of Nazareth passing by, he began to shout: *"Jesus, Son of David, have mercy on me!" (Mark 10:47.NLT)*

The crowd tried to silence him, but Bartimaeus cried out even louder, desperate for Jesus' attention and healing:

"Son of David, have mercy on me!" (Mark 10:48, NLT)

Jesus did not ignore his desperate and persistent cry. In verse forty-nine, Jesus stopped and called Bartimaeus to Him. When Bartimaeus came, Jesus asked him what he wanted, and Bartimaeus replied that he wanted to see. Jesus responded:

"Go, for your faith has healed you." (Mark 10:52, NLT)

Immediately, Bartimaeus received his sight and followed Jesus along the road. This story illustrates the power of a desperate cry to Jesus. Bartimaeus' persistence, despite the crowd's attempts to silence him, reflects the importance of crying out to God in faith, even in desperate circumstances. His determination and faith were rewarded with healing and restoration.

Cry of faith: The Roman Officer with the sick servant

An example of a cry of faith in the Bible can be seen in the story of the Roman centurion who sought Jesus to heal his sick servant. This account is in Luke 7:1-10 and Matthew 8:5-13. The centurion, a Roman officer, had a highly valued servant who was sick and near death.

Despite being a Gentile and not a Jew, the centurion displayed a remarkable faith in Jesus' power to heal. Instead of demanding or begging, the centurion sent Jewish elders to Jesus, asking for his help, and later, when Jesus was on His way to his home, the centurion sent friends to deliver a message:

"Lord, don't trouble yourself by coming to my home, for I am not worthy of such an honor. I am not even worthy to come and meet you. Just say the word from where you are, and my servant will be healed." (Luke 7:6-7, NLT)

This statement of faith amazed Jesus, who said:

- o *"I tell you, I haven't seen faith like this in all Israel!"*
  (Luke 7:9, NLT)

The centurion believed that Jesus could heal his servant with just a word, demonstrating his deep faith in Jesus' authority and power. Jesus honored this faith, and when the friends returned to the centurion's house, they found the servant healed. This story highlights how a cry of faith, even from someone outside the Jewish faith, moved Jesus to act. The centurion's faith was not only strong but also humble, recognizing Jesus' authority without needing His physical presence. This cry of faith resulted in the miraculous healing of his servant.

Prophetic Cry: a combination of the misunderstood and desperate cry. Isaiah 6:1-8 describes how the train of Gods glory filled the temple.

A powerful example of a prophetic cry that combines both a misunderstanding and a desperate cry is in Isaiah 6:1-8. In this passage, the prophet Isaiah experiences a profound vision of God, which leads him to cry out in recognition of his unworthiness and the overwhelming holiness of God.

The Scene: A Vision of God's Glory

Isaiah sees the Lord seated on a high and exalted throne, with the train of His robe filling the temple. This imagery of the train filling the temple symbolizes the fullness of God's glory and presence. Seraphim are present, calling out, "Holy, holy, holy is the Lord of Heaven's Armies! The whole earth is filled with his glory!" *(Isaiah 6:3, NLT)*. The temple shakes, and it is filled with smoke.

The Cry: Misunderstood and Desperate

Isaiah's response to this vision is a cry of desperation and recognition of his sinfulness:

- o "Woe to me!" I cried. "I am ruined! For I am a man of unclean lips, and I live among a people of unclean lips, and my eyes have seen the King, the Lord Almighty." *(Isaiah 6:5, NLT)*

Isaiah's cry is desperate, overwhelmed by both the holiness of God and his own unworthiness to stand in His presence. Isaiah misunderstands, as he initially sees his situation as hopeless—feeling undone and unworthy, not yet understanding the cleansing, and commissioning that God has prepared for him.

The Cleansing and Commissioning

In response to Isaiah's cry, one of the seraphim flies to him with a live coal taken from the altar and touches his lips, saying, "See, this has touched your lips; your guilt is taken away and your sin atoned for." *(Isaiah 6:7, NLT)*

Isaiah's cry leads to a profound transformation. What he thought was a moment of judgment becomes a moment of purification and commissioning. God then asks, "Whom shall I send? And who will go for us?" *(Isaiah 6:8a, NLT)*

Isaiah, now cleansed and emboldened, responds with another prophetic cry, this time one of willingness and readiness:
o "Here I am. Send me!" *(Isaiah 6:8b, NLT)*

This passage shows how a prophetic cry can arise from deep desperation and a feeling of being misunderstood, leading to a greater revelation of God's purpose. Isaiah's experience shows that when we bring our deepest fears and feelings of inadequacy to God, He can transform them into a powerful calling, using us as vessels for His divine mission.

Creation crying for the sons of God to be revealed

An example of creation crying out for the sons of God to be revealed can be found in Romans 8:19-22 (NLT) :
o "For all creation is waiting eagerly for that future day when God will reveal who his children really are. Against its will, all creation was subjected to God's curse. But with eager hope, the creation looks forward to the day when it will join God's children in glorious freedom from death and decay.

For we know that all creation has been groaning as in the pains of childbirth right up to the present time."

Explanation:

o Creation's Groaning: Paul uses the metaphor of creation "groaning" as in childbirth, which conveys a deep, collective longing for renewal and restoration. This groaning represents the suffering and brokenness present in the world as a result of sin, which affected not just humanity but all of creation.

o Sons of God to Be Revealed: The "sons of God" refers to those who are God's children, the believers who will be revealed and glorified when Christ returns. Creation eagerly anticipates this revelation because it is tied to the hope of its own redemption.

o Restoration and Redemption: The passage suggests that creation is currently in a state of decay and suffering, but it holds on to the hope of being liberated from this state when the sons of God are revealed. This reflects a cosmic hope, not just for humanity but for all of God's creation to be restored to its intended glory.

Application:

This passage is often cited in discussions about the impact of sin on the natural world and the broader theme of redemption and restoration in Christian eschatology. It speaks to the interconnectedness of all creation with humanity's destiny and the ultimate hope of renewal through God's redemptive plan.

Scriptures about crying

- "Lord, I cry out to You; Make haste to me! Give ear to my voice when I cry out to You. Let my prayer be set before You as incense, The lifting up of my hands as the evening sacrifice." *(Psalms 141:1-2)*

- "You have kept a record of my wanderings. Put my tears in your bottle. They are already in your book. Then my enemies will retreat when I call to you. This I know: God is on my side." *(Psalm 56:8-9)*

- "Then they cried to the LORD in their trouble, and he saved them from their distress." *(Psalm 107:19)*

- "The righteous cry out, and the LORD hears them; he delivers them from all their troubles." *(Psalm 34:17)*

- o "Then they cried out to the LORD in their trouble, and he delivered them from their distress." *(Psalm 107:6)*

- o "Don't worry about anything; instead, pray about everything. Tell God what you need, and thank him for all he has done. And the peace of God, which transcends all understanding, will guard your hearts and your minds in Christ Jesus." *(Philippians 4:6-7)*

- o "God is our protection and source of strength. He is always ready to help us in times of trouble." *(Psalm 46:1)*

God Hears us When we cry or pray

- o "In my distress I called to the LORD; I cried to my God for help. From his temple he heard my voice; my cry came before him, into his ears." *(Psalm 18:6)*

- o "In my alarm I said, "I am cut off from your sight!" Yet you heard my cry for mercy when I called to you for help." *(Psalm 31:22)*

- o "He will fulfill the desire of them that fear him: he also will hear their cry, and will save them." *(Psalm 145:19)*

- "Lord, you know the hopes of the helpless. Surely you will hear their cries and comfort them." *(Psalm 10:17)*
- "The eyes of the Lord watch over those who do right; his ears are open to their cries for help." *(Psalm 34:15)*

The righteous have a watchman over their prayers. He protects, keeps an eye on, observes, attends, watches, and follows. He is always listening to our prayers. The lord sets his focus and attention on those who do his will, obey, and surrender to him.

- "In my desperation I prayed, and the Lord listened; he saved me from all my troubles." *(Psalm 34:6)*

"In desperate times our only response should be prayer!" – *Shavaunta Harris*

He Understands the Language of Tears

God understands the language of tears. The Bible tells us in Psalm 56:8 (NLT), "You keep track of all my sorrows. You have collected all my tears in your bottle. You have recorded each one in your book." This verse beautifully illustrates how deeply God cares for us, even to the point of capturing every tear we shed. Our tears are significant to Him; they are a powerful form of communication that transcends words.

From a clinical perspective, crying has been shown to have tangible benefits. Research from Harvard indicates that crying releases oxytocin and endorphins—natural chemicals in our bodies that help alleviate both physical and emotional pain. These "feel-good" chemicals can create a sense of relief and emotional cleansing, helping us to process difficult feelings.

Now, imagine the profound impact of releasing those tears in prayer before our Holy God. When we cry out to Him, we are not only letting go of our burdens, but also opening ourselves to receive His comfort, strength, and peace. Our tears, mingled with prayer, become a conduit for God's healing presence in our lives.

Have you ever felt the weight of life so heavy that it seems unbearable? Overwhelmed, frustrated, and downright exhausted, you might have tried everything to find relief—scheduling a massage, reading a book, taking a nap—only to discover that nothing worked. I have been there too. But it was not until I cried out to the Lord in prayer that I found the peace and comfort for which I was searching.

Psalm 120:1 (NLT) says, "I took my troubles to the Lord; I cried out to him, and he answered my prayer." In this verse, David gives us a profound truth: when we feel overwhelmed, stressed, or burdened by life's challenges, the answer is to cry out to the Lord in prayer. It is in these moments of vulnerability that God meets us, hears our unspoken words through our tears, and responds with His loving kindness.

So, if you find yourself in a place where words fail and all you have left are tears, know that God understands. He sees each tear and hears the cry of your heart. Your tears are not just a release—they are a prayer, a deep expression of your need for God's presence. And He is faithful to answer, bringing the comfort, peace, and strength that only He can provide.

Waiting in God's presence

Waiting is a significant part of the believer's journey, especially in the place of prayer. We often find ourselves waiting—waiting for God to move, waiting for Him to answer, waiting for His timing. It is in this place of waiting that many experience frustration, anger, confusion, and sometimes even the temptation to give up on God. The challenge of waiting can make it feel like anything but a blessing. Yet, when we truly grasp that God's timing is perfect, we begin to see the beauty in the waiting. It becomes a time of deepening trust, where our faith is tested and refined.

The Bible is filled with examples of people who had to wait on God. Abraham waited for the promise of Isaac. Joseph waited in prison for his dreams to be fulfilled.

The Israelites waited 40 years to enter the Promised Land. Even the early disciples waited in the Upper Room for the Holy Spirit to come. In each instance, God's timing proved to be perfect, and His answers far exceeded what they could have imagined.

In our own lives, waiting on God often feels like an arduous task. Sometimes, our words fail us. We cannot even begin to express what is happening within our hearts and lives. But we are not left alone in these moments. Jesus understands our struggles and needs. As Matthew 6:8 reminds us, "Your Father knows exactly what you need even before you ask him."

There are times when we are so overwhelmed that we don't know what to pray for. In these moments, the Holy Spirit intercedes for us. Romans 8:26 (NLT) says, "And the Holy Spirit helps us in our weakness. For example, we don't know what God wants us to pray for. But the Holy Spirit prays for us with groanings that cannot be expressed in words." This divine help is a gift. The Holy Spirit steps in, praying through us and for us when our own words fall short.

Waiting may not be easy, but it is in the waiting that God shapes our character, strengthens our faith, and prepares us for the answers to come. So, when you find yourself in a season of waiting, remember that God is at work. He is not ignoring your prayers; He is preparing you for the right moment. Trust in His timing, lean into His presence, and allow the Holy Spirit to guide your heart and prayers as you wait on the Lord.

An Effective Prayer life

As people of His presence, we must have an appetite and hunger for HIM, HIS word, and HIS will. In order to see the fruit in our life of answered prayer, we must know that only God can answer our prayer, only God can provide for us and only God satisfies us. Do not misunderstand what I am saying here, God can use people to be vessels for His will to be accomplished but we must always remember that it is God who answers prayer not people. If we tried to define what effective prayer looks like in today's modern Christianity, all we'd need to do is scroll through our favorite social media platform. There, we'd quickly see how today's culture has come to define it.

We are bombarded with pre-planned, pre-curated, man-made desires fulfilled by man, and then dressed in the name of Christ, as if God were the one behind the desire. We have an extreme growth of believers that have perpetuated a false narrative of what answered and effective prayer looks like.

Many have given into the idea that we can move ahead of God, skip praying and go with what we think is right, create the result we want and then look to God, ask Him to bless this because this is what we want. Then we present it on social media as if God has answered our prayers.

No! This is not the way of our Father! What we see happening today in the hearts of God's people is a performative and selfish desire to be noticed, seen and accepted by people rather than God!
Isaiah 55:8-9 "My thoughts are nothing like your thoughts," says the Lord. "And my ways are far beyond anything you could imagine. For just as the heavens are higher than the earth, so my ways are higher than your ways and my thoughts higher than your thoughts."

What these few verses explain to us is that God's wisdom surpasses human understanding. His plans and purposes are beyond human comprehension, and what He does or allows may not always make sense to us, but it is always part of His greater and wiser plan. He also encourages us to trust Him: Since God's thoughts and ways are higher, we are encouraged to trust Him, even when we do not understand His actions or timing.

Lastly, God calls us to align with His will: understanding that God's ways are higher than ours should lead us to seek alignment with His will, abandoning our limited and often flawed perspectives. This should encourage us to seek God earnestly knowing that what He has planned for us is greater.

We should want what God wants for us, pray for what God wants for us and believe that God will do what He says concerning us. When we chase after our will, we will have to work hard to make it happen. I don't know about you, but I have never known anyone to outwork God.

We must be able to submit ourselves to God. We will not succeed in anything apart from God! God has already ordered our steps. Our focus should be to seek Him, ask Him, and obey Him. It is YOUR vision, YOUR work or HIS vision, HIS work. This brings me to my next point, trusting Him enough to submit to His will.

Submission is a topic that may cause some people problems. Mature believers know and understand that this is exactly what Jesus modeled all throughout His time in ministry. Being submissive or the lack thereof has consequences and sometimes those consequences can lead to our spiritual death.

Pray like your life depends on it!

"God desires for His promises in your life to be brought to pass through your participation in prayer." – Shavaunta Harris

---

Your prayer life is not only an essential part of your spiritual journey—it is your divine mandate as a believer. The choice is simple: you will either pray or become prey. You will either use the powerful gift of prayer or choose not to. But remember, it's not just your life that hangs in the balance—someone else's breakthrough, healing, or salvation may depend on your prayers. So, never stop praying! Never cease to call on the name of your Father, lifting Him up in every situation. PRAY UNTIL SOMETHING HAPPENS...and if nothing happens, keep on praying until it does!

I want to leave you with three simple, but powerful instructions: keep asking, keep seeking, and keep knocking. Prayer is less about the answers and more about deepening your intimacy with God. So, press in, persevere, and watch how your life—and the lives of those around you—are transformed through the power of persistent prayer.

Come back to this book often. Use it as a tool to guide you, to reignite your passion, and to share with others who need encouragement in their prayer journey. Make a commitment to God and to yourself that you will not be a casualty of unanswered prayer. Keep praying, keep believing, and watch as God moves mightily in your life.

As we are near the end of this book, my hope is that it has served as a catalyst to ignite your prayer life. Every tool shared within these pages is meant to equip and empower you to deepen your intimacy with God and strengthen your connection with other believers. Jesus invites us in John 17 to be one with the Father as He is one with Him—a profound call to unity and communion through prayer. I pray that you embrace this invitation wholeheartedly, committing to pray through all things, no matter the circumstances. Pray like your life depends on it because it truly does!

CHAPTER 7

PRAYERS AND DECLARATIONS

Now, it is time to put into practice what we have explored. This chapter is designed to equip you with practical tools, prayers, and decrees that will help you on your journey of prayer. Whether you are just beginning or seeking to deepen your prayer life, these resources are intended to guide and support you every step of the way.

You will find clear definitions to help you understand key concepts, alongside powerful prayer decrees that can be spoken over your life and circumstances. These decrees are not just words, but declarations rooted in scripture, designed to align your heart with God's promises and activate His power in your life.

Additionally, I have included various prayers that you can use as a starting point or as a source of inspiration in your personal time with God. These prayers are meant to be flexible tools that you can adapt and personalize to fit your unique situation. They are crafted to help you engage in meaningful conversation with God, drawing you closer to Him and deepening your relationship.

Prayer is not just discipline; it is a journey that grows and evolves with time. The tools and teachings provided here are meant to help you continue growing, not just in prayer, but in faith, confidence, and spiritual authority.

As you work through these resources, I encourage you to allow the Holy Spirit to lead you. He will guide and teach you as you seek to grow in your prayer life. May these tools empower you to step into your God-given authority, deepen your connection with Him, and see His hand move mightily in every area of your life.

Remember, this is just the beginning. Let these prayers, decrees, and teachings be a foundation upon which you continue to build a life of powerful and effective prayer.

Definition of Declaration:

What does it mean to declare? The definition of a declaration means "to make known," "set forth," it is spoken from a place of power and authority. In order to understand a declaration, I want to give an example of a king and his servants. When you think back to the days kings made decrees, they would write them down, then be given to their servants to speak and declare to the people on behalf of the king. People would obey because of the authority of the person who wrote the decree. This is the same for us as believers. We are servants of the King of Kings, the most-High God!

We have a right because we belong to God to declare what has already been written or decreed by our King in the Word of God. There is an authority and power that we have, not because of us but because of the power in the God we serve. When these servants spoke, they did not speak the declarations hoping that what they said would be done or enforced. They spoke knowing that every word spoken not only had power, but would cause some things to change immediately as soon as it came from their mouths. That is the same power and authority that you have because of the blood of Jesus Christ.

The bible says in Job 22:28-30, "You will also declare a thing, And it will be established for you; So light will shine on your ways. When they cast you down, and you say, 'Exaltation will come!' Then He will save the humble person. He will even deliver one who is not innocent; Yes, he will be delivered by the purity of your hands."

Open your mouth and begin to declare these powerful declarations over your life. As you speak out these scriptures ask God to remove any doubt in your heart. The Word of God spoken out of the mouth of a believer is powerful but only where there is faith attached! Hebrews 4:12 "For the word of God is alive and active. Sharper than any double-edged sword, it penetrates even to dividing soul and spirit, joints and marrow; it judges the thoughts and attitudes of the heart." The Word of God is all you need coupled with your faith to declare victory over your life. Deliverance is something that can take time.

Come back to this section as often as you need to, daily if needed. I am praying that these declarations not just change your situation but most of all CHANGE YOU! Before you begin praying these declarations and decrees over your life, I want to help you understand by giving you seven definitions first.

1. **Denounce:** to give formal notice of termination or denial: condemn.

2. **Rebuke:** sharp stern disapproval, reprimand.

3. **Renounce:** to disown, to give up or put aside voluntarily or give up by formal declaration.

4. **Cast out (eckballow):** to drive out or impel by violence, to throw, fling, or send; that is, to drive from, by force.

5. **Confession:** to own, acknowledge or avow, as a crime, a fault; a charge, a debt, or something that is against one's interest, or reputation. To acknowledge sins and faults.

6. **Declaration:** make known; to tell explicitly; to manifest or communicate plainly to others by words.

7. **Decree:** to determine or resolve legislatively; to fix or appoint; to set or constitute by edict or in purpose. In theology, predetermined purpose of God; the purpose or determination of an immutable being, whose plan of operations is, like himself, unchangeable.

"Thou shalt also decree a thing, and it shall be established unto thee: and the light shall shine upon thy ways.." (Job 22:28, KJV)

Prayers of Repentance

Before we begin praying we want to approach God with a repentant heart and seek him for forgiveness. Pray this prayer of faith and repentance! "Search me, O God, and know my heart; test me and know my anxious thoughts. Point out anything in me that offends you, and lead me along the path of everlasting life." *(Psalm 139:23-24)*

Father, grant me the faith to trust in Your Word and to pray it boldly. Your Word assures that it will never return empty, for You are faithful and true. Sometimes, Lord, it feels like my faith wavers, but what I truly need is a deeper intimacy with You, so I can speak Your promises with unwavering confidence. Strengthen my belief, Lord, and help me overcome any doubts I may have. When weariness sets in, and doubts creep in, revive my faith, breathe new life into it until it is fully restored.

Remind me, Lord, of the prayers I have offered in faith, and empower me to cling to Your promises until I witness Your mighty hand at work. Your word says that unrepented sin could hinder my prayers (Psalm 66:18).

Father, I ask for forgiveness of any unconfessed sin in my life, and I forgive anyone who has caused pain in my life physically, spiritual, mentally, and emotionally. Set me free from the snare of every enemy and help me to acknowledge the power given to me through Jesus. Grant me the grace to stand firm on Your Word, knowing that Your promises are true. In Jesus' name, I pray and believe,

Amen.

Prayer for the Lords Help

Heavenly Father, I come before You seeking Your help. Help me in my heart, my mind, my understanding, and in my waiting. Help me in all that You have called me to do. Father, stir in me a desire for the deep relationship with You that You have always longed to have with me. I admit there have been many moments of uncertainty in my life. I have doubted my own abilities and struggled to fully believe in You. Right now, as I pray, I ask that You help me believe in the power of Your Word concerning prayer.

Your Word tells us in 1 John 5:14-15, "We are confident that He hears us whenever we ask for anything that pleases Him. And since we know He hears us when we make our requests, we also know that He will give us what we ask for."

Lord, help me to be consistent in prayer and to trust You fully with my life. Guide me as I grow in my devotion and understanding of what it means to pray without ceasing. Search my heart, Lord, for any doubt, anger, anxiety, fear, unforgiveness, guilt, shame, worry, or malice, and remove anything that stands in the way of You speaking to me and accomplishing Your will in my life.

Father, give me a heart of prayer. I long to be in complete fellowship and relationship with You. Thank You in advance for the growth, the strength, and most of all, the transformation that You will bring about in me. In Jesus name,

Amen.

Prayer of Salvation

Heavenly Father, I come to You in need of Your grace and mercy. I know that I am a sinner and have made mistakes. Your Word says in Romans 3:23, "For all have sinned and fall short of the glory of God." I admit that I have sinned and need Your forgiveness.

You sent Your Son, Jesus Christ, to die for my sins. John 3:16 tells me, "For God so loved the world that He gave His one and only Son, that whoever believes in Him shall not perish but have eternal life." Jesus died on the cross for me and rose again on the third day, just as it says in 1 Corinthians 15:3-4, "Christ died for our sins…He was buried, and He was raised on the third day according to the Scriptures."

Lord Jesus, I ask You to come into my heart and be my Lord and Savior. I want to turn away from my sins and follow You. Romans 10:9 says, "If you declare with your mouth, 'Jesus is Lord,' and believe in your heart that God raised Him from the dead, you will be saved." I declare that Jesus is Lord, and God raised Him from the dead.

Please forgive me for all my sins and help me to live a new life in You. I ask for Your Holy Spirit to guide me, teach me, and help me grow in my faith. Your Word promises in 1 John 1:9, "If we confess our sins, He is faithful and just and will forgive us our sins and purify us from all unrighteousness."

Thank You, Lord, for loving me, for forgiving me, and for giving me a new life in Christ. I am now a child of God, and I trust in You for all my days. In Jesus' name, I pray,

Amen.

Declaration of Faith

Prayer and faith are connected! Your faithfulness in prayer will unlock blessings. The attack on your prayer life is directly linked to your faith.

Father in the name of Jesus I come before you seeking out your desire for my life. Father I repent of every place in my heart that I have doubted you, every place where I did not believe and did not trust you. Lord, help my unbelief, give me the faith to trust you even when it does not make sense. Thank you Lord for another opportunity to draw closer to you and to understand more about you and your character. Your word says in Matthew 7:7, "ask and it will be given to you seek and you will find knock and the door will be open to you."

Today, I am asking that you increase my faith. Give me a greater revelation of what faith really is as I pray and seek your face. As I read and study your Word, remind me of what it says about faith.

- o "Now faith is the substance of things hoped for and the evidence of things not seen." *(Hebrews 11:1)*
- o "And Jesus answering saith unto them, Have faith in God." *(Mark 11:22)*
- o "For we live by faith not by sight." *(2 Corinthians 5:7)*

- o "Because you know that the testing of your faith produces perseverance." *(James 1:3)*
- o "So that your faith might not rest on human wisdom, but on God's power." *(1 Corinthians 2:5)*
- o "The apostles said to the Lord, Increase our faith!" *(Luke 17:5)*
- o "Without faith it's impossible to please God." *(Hebrews 11:6)*
- o "Whatever you ask for in prayer, believe that you have received it, and it will be yours." *(Mark 11:24)*
- o "Consequently, faith comes by hearing and hearing by the word of God." *(Romans 10:17)*
- o "For it is by grace that we have been saved, through faith-and this is not from yourselves, it is the gift of God." *(Ephesians 2:8)*

Lord Help me to believe in your word that says, "you will withhold no good thing from those that walk upright," according to Psalm 84:11. My desire is that I have faith that speaks to my situation. No matter what I am going through I trust your word. Lord, I am declaring I have the faith to believe. I have asked and you have heard. Now I seal this prayer with praise in faith that no word from God will ever fail, according to Luke 1:37.

This is my prayer in Jesus name,

Amen.

Declaration of the Power of the Blood of Jesus

As the disciples sat together, Jesus said, "Take this and eat it, for this is my body." And he took a cup of wine and gave thanks to God for it. He gave it to them and said, "Each of you drink from it, for this is my blood, which confirms the covenant between God and his people. It is poured out as a sacrifice to forgive the sins of many.

o   Matthew 26:26-28.

The blood of Jesus symbolizes the cleansing of sin. As you speak this declaration over your life know that the blood of Jesus has power to cleanse you of all sin, iniquity, and all unrighteousness. As you pray this declaration I want to speak over you that everything that has been holding you up, hindering your growth and blocking you from victory is destroyed by the power of the blood of Jesus Christ. You are declared free because of the price that was paid by Jesus Christ! You have power over everything that has been coming against you and because of the blood of Jesus Christ YOU can declare victory!

Here are seven applications of the blood of Jesus in your life. I urge you to pray these scriptures and make these declarations daily. There is power in knowing and applying these powerful truths about the blood of Jesus that grants you access to freedom in Christ!

Declaring the Seven Applications of the Blood of Jesus

1. **Redemption: Ephesians 1:7, I Peter 1:18-19, Psalm 107:2**

   Confession: "Through the blood of Jesus, I have been redeemed out of the hand of the Devil."

2. **Cleansing: I John 1:7; Psalm 51**

   Confession: "While I walk in the Light, the Blood of Jesus cleanses me now and continually for all sin."

3. **Justification: Romans 5:9, Isaiah 61:10**

   Confession: "Through the Blood of Jesus, I am justified, acquitted, not guilty, reckoned righteous, made righteous just as if I never sinned."

4. **Sanctification: Hebrews 13:12**

   Confession: "Through the Blood of Jesus, I am sanctified, made holy, set apart to God, separated from sin, made holy with God's Holiness."

5. **Life: Leviticus 17:11, John 6:53-57, I Corinthians 10:16; 11:23 (Communion)**

   Confession: "Lord Jesus, when we receive your Blood, we receive Your Life...the Life of God, Divine, Eternal, and Endless. Thank you Lord."

6. **Intercession: Hebrews 12:22-24**

   Confession: " Thank you Lord that even when I cannot pray the Blood of Jesus is pleading for me in Heaven."

7. **Access: Hebrews 10:19-23; 3:1; 4:14**

   And they overcame him by the blood of the Lamb, and by the word of their testimony; and they loved not their lives unto the death. - Revelation 12:11 (KJV)

Prayer Confession of the Blood of Jesus

Confession: "Thank you Lord that through the sprinkled Blood of Jesus, I have access into the Presence of Almighty God, the holiest place in the universe." I stand in the power of the blood of Jesus in my life.

o   My debt of sin is paid, once and for all. (Hebrews 9:28)

o   I am justified. (Romans 5:9)

o   I am forgiven. (Ephesians 1:7)

o   I am spared from God's wrath. (Romans 5:9)

o   I am spiritually alive. (John 6:35)

o   My judgment is satisfied, and I am at peace with God. (Isaiah 53:5)

o   I have the power to overcome the enemy. (Revelation 12:11)

o   I have been reclaimed from the enemy. (Ephesians 1:7)

o   I am no longer under the curse of the law. (Galatians 3:13)

o   I am no longer a stranger to the covenant of promise. (Ephesians 2:12-13)

- o I have been translated from the enemy's kingdom to God's kingdom. (Colossians 2:15)
- o I have access to the unmerited favor of God. (Ephesians 1:7)
- o I am justified, as though I have never sinned. (Romans 3:24-25)
- o My redemption will never perish. (1 Peter 1:18-19)
- o Jesus testifies on my behalf that I am clean. (Revelation 1:5)
- o I am free. (Galatians 5:1)
- o I am free from a conscience defiled by guilt. (Hebrews 10:22)
- o I can proclaim victory. (Revelation 12:11)
- o I have a revelation of God. (Hebrews 10:19-22)

I speak these scriptures in power and in faith that the blood of Jesus gives me power and strength and I seal this declaration in faith in my life in Jesus name!

Declaration for Healing

Father, in the name of Jesus, I thank You, Lord, for the power of Your word. I know full well the healing power Your word holds. Just as You spoke the world into existence in Genesis, so it is with Your word today. As I pray this declaration of healing over my mind, body, spirit, and soul, I believe, by the power of Your word, that I am healed. Your word says in Isaiah 53:5, "By His stripes we are healed," and I claim that healing over my life. Through the blood of Jesus, I am free from all sickness and disease.

By the power of the blood of Jesus, sickness and disease are far from me! I declare that I am healed from childhood trauma, abuse, molestation, verbal abuse, mental abuse, and all forms of emotional and physical torture. I am healed from unspeakable pain, from hurtful words, and from word curses spoken knowingly or unknowingly over my life. In Psalm 107:20, Your word says, "He sent out His word and healed them; He rescued them from the grave," and I stand on that promise for my healing.

I declare that I am healed from any sexually transmitted diseases, autoimmune diseases, kidney diseases, bone diseases, blood diseases, infectious diseases, deficiency diseases, hereditary diseases (both genetic and non-genetic), and psychological diseases.

Your word says in Jeremiah 30:17, "For I will restore health to you, and your wounds I will heal," and I claim this restoration in every area of my life.

I decree and declare that I am free from all manner of sickness and disease, and by the power of the Holy Spirit and the blood of Jesus, I am healed, delivered, and set free. I speak healing over emotional wounds, the wounds to my ego, and any harm to my confidence. In 2 Timothy 1:7, Your word says, "For God has not given us a spirit of fear, but of power, love, and a sound mind," and I declare a sound mind over myself, free from the effects of emotional abuse and control.

I break and destroy all emotional abuse tied to controlling, degrading, undermining, and manipulative behaviors. In Galatians 5:1, Your word says, "It is for freedom that Christ has set us free; stand firm, then, and do not let yourselves be burdened again by a yoke of slavery," and I declare that I am free from all patterns of manipulation and control in my life. I sever the ties of passive-aggressive behavior and demonic control. I break free from judgment, lies, blaming, name-calling, ordering, raging, and criticism disguised as jokes, as well as any form of jealousy.

- I am healed by stripes of Jesus. (Isaiah 53:5)
- I am healed of a broken heart. (Psalms 147:3)
- I am healed from all kinds of sicknesses and diseases. (Matthew 4:23)
- I am healed from head to toe. (Proverbs 3:8)

According to your word I am set free, healed, and delivered by the power of the blood of Jesus. In Jesus' name,

I declare my freedom and healing!

Amen.

Declaration for Deliverance

Through the blood of Jesus, I am born again and declared free from every sin and its effects. As it says in Revelation 1:5, "To him who loves us and has freed us from our sins by his blood," I am no longer bound by sin. Satan has no power over me and no place in me. I will not be oppressed, suppressed, or depressed in any way. Psalm 18:2 declares, "The Lord is my rock, my fortress, and my deliverer; my God is my rock, in whom I take refuge, my shield and the horn of my salvation, my stronghold." I run to the safety of His name in the midst of trouble.

I have the truth of the Word of God within me. Jesus said in John 8:32, "Then you will know the truth, and the truth will set you free," and I stand in that freedom. I am walking in the finished work of Jesus Christ, seated in heavenly places with Him, as Ephesians 2:6 declares, "And God raised us up with Christ and seated us with him in the heavenly realms in Christ Jesus." My name is written in the Lamb's book of life, and Jesus knows me by name, just as John 10:3 says, "He calls his own sheep by name and leads them out."

I have been given power and authority over darkness, as Luke 10:19 states, "I have given you authority to trample on snakes and scorpions and to overcome all the power of the enemy; nothing will harm you."

I am delivered from all my troubles, according to Psalm 34:17, "The righteous cry out, and the Lord hears them; he delivers them from all their troubles." I am free from all distress, as Psalm 107:6 says, "Then they cried out to the Lord in their trouble, and He delivered them from their distress."

I am free from the oppression of any demon and from addictions to drugs, alcohol, smoking, food, gambling, abortions, sex, pornography, and masturbation. I declare freedom from all demonic spirits of perversion. I am also free from the effects of molestation, murder, deeply rooted grief, pain, cutting, suicidal attempts and thoughts, rape, and crime. Galatians 5:1 reminds me, "It is for freedom that Christ has set us free; stand firm, then, and do not let yourselves be burdened again by a yoke of slavery."

I bind the strong man and cast out the root spirits of divination, the spirit of jealousy, familiar spirits, lying spirits, perverse spirits, the spirit of haughtiness, the spirit of heaviness, the spirit of whoredoms, the spirit of infirmity, the deaf and dumb spirit, the spirit of bondage, the spirit of fear, seducing spirits, the spirit of the antichrist, the spirit of error, the spirit of poverty, and the spirit of death. Matthew 18:18 says, "Truly I tell you, whatever you bind on earth will be bound in heaven, and whatever you loose on earth will be loosed in heaven." Matthew 12:29 affirms, "How can anyone enter a strong man's house and carry off his possessions unless he first ties up the strong man?"

I confess my sins and the effects of these demonic spirits, and I renounce all allegiance to them. I receive the fullness of Your forgiveness through Christ's blood, as 1 John 1:9 declares, "If we confess our sins, He is faithful and just to forgive us our sins and to cleanse us from all unrighteousness." I declare that the old has passed away, and I am made new in Christ, as 2 Corinthians 5:17 says, "Therefore, if anyone is in Christ, the new creation has come: The old has gone, the new is here!"

I have the mind of Christ, as 1 Corinthians 2:16 declares, "But we have the mind of Christ." I am seated in heavenly places with Christ Jesus, free indeed, as John 8:36 says, "So if the Son sets you free, you will be free indeed." I have overcome evil with good, as it is written in Romans 12:21, "Do not be overcome by evil, but overcome evil with good."

By the authority of the blood of Jesus, I receive deliverance and healing. Isaiah 53:5 reminds me, "By His stripes we are healed." I stand in this victory and declare that I am healed, delivered, and set free in Jesus' name. Amen!

Declaration for Identity

For so long, I lived much of my childhood and early adult life with my identity under constant attack. I realized that as long as I remained blind to the truth of who I was in Christ, I lived beneath my privilege. I accepted less and often did not expect the best in my life. But when I received the revelation of being a child of God and gained an understanding of sonship and being a joint heir with Christ, everything changed. I discovered whose I was, which in turn allowed me to accept who I was.

I want to share with you that this can be true for you as well. I encourage you to meditate on scriptures about your identity in Christ! The root of many identity issues is the spirit of rejection. Man may have rejected you, but I want you to know you have been accepted by God. You must receive the revelation of who you are to God and understand your sonship in Him.

Your identity will always come under attack by the enemy because he knows that a blind believer yields no power.

But a believer who sees themselves as they truly are in Christ wields the same power that raised Christ from the grave. A believer with God's perspective of themselves is a threat to Satan. God wants you to know not only who you are but whose you are. You must understand that you have been bought with a price, and God has established your identity and your value in His kingdom. He calls you priceless!

I decree and declare that you have the DNA of Christ. I agree with the Word of God that says I am made in His image. I take on the full image of Christ and I walk in my kingdom authority in Christ Jesus! I decree over my life that I am who you say I am.

I cast out every area in my life of identity confusion, identity theft, identity crises, loss of my sense of identity, loss of my self-worth, self-esteem, self-awareness, self-image, perfectionism, people pleasing, being performance driven, walking in the shadow of a spouse, sibling or friend, comparison, unrealistic expectations, fear of rejection, lack of support, perceiving myself as being unworthy, lack of acceptance of the real me and anything that has come to distort and destroy my kingdom identity.

Every area of misplaced identity, I speak against every spirit that has attempted to steal my identity. I come against every area in your mind that would cause you to forget who God has created you to be. We break down every lie of the enemy. We speak against the spirit of rejection. I step in to my rightful place in you! I accept my God given identity in Jesus Christ through the blood of Jesus!

Scriptures to Pray for Identity:

"We know that our old self [our human nature without the Holy Spirit] was nailed to the cross with Him, in order that our body of sin might be done away with, so that we would no longer be slaves to sin." *(Romans 6:6 AMP)*

- "But to all who believed him and accepted him, he gave the right to become children of God." *(John 1:12)*
- "God decided in advance to adopt us into his own family by bringing us to himself through Jesus Christ. This is what he wanted to do, and it gave him great pleasure." *(Ephesians 1:5)*
- "Therefore, accept each other just as Christ has accepted you so that God will be given glory." (Romans 15:7)
- "For in Christ lives all the fullness of God in a human body. So you also are complete through your union with Christ, who is the head over every ruler and authority." *(Colossians 2:9-10)*
- "But the person who is joined to the Lord is one spirit with him." *(1 Corinthians 6:17)*
- "So God created human beings in his own image. In the image of God he created them; male and female he created them." *(Genesis 1:27)*

o "I knew you before I formed you in your mother's womb. Before you were born I set you apart and appointed you as my prophet to the nations." (Jeremiah 1:5)

o "But you are not like that, for you are a chosen people. You are royal priests, a holy nation, God's very own possession. As a result, you can show others the goodness of God, for he called you out of the darkness into his wonderful light." *(1 Peter 2:9)*

o "See how very much our Father loves us, for he calls us his children, and that is what we are! But the people who belong to this world don't recognize that we are God's children because they don't know him. Dear friends, we are already God's children, but he has not yet shown us what we will be like when Christ appears. But we do know that we will be like him, for we will see him as he really is." *(1 John 3:1-2)*

o "And you belong to Christ, and Christ belongs to God." *(1 Corinthians 3:23)*

o "So do not throw away this confident trust in the Lord. Remember the great reward it brings you!" *(Hebrews 10:35)*

Declaration for Provision

I decree and declare that God's hand of provision is upon my life.

- o I have an abundant life. (John 10:10)
- o All of my help comes from God, and I lack nothing. (Psalm 23:1)
- o God is able to bless me abundantly. God is able to bless me in all things at all times, I have all that I need, and I will abound in every good work. (2 Corinthians 9:8)
- o God has given me everything I need for a godly life through my knowledge of him who called me by his glory and goodness. (2 Peter 1:3)
- o My god will meet all my needs according to his riches and glory in Christ Jesus. (Phillippians4:19)
- o My confidence and trust are in God and therefore I am blessed. (Jeremiah 17:7)
- o God's provision is on my food and water. (Exodus 23:25)
- o I am filled with the good of the land and the blessings of the lord shall be my portion.
- o I will see the goodness of the Lord in the land of the living. (psalm 27:13)
- o I declare I am never dry, never fainting, ever blessed and ever prosperous because I am meditating on the word of the Lord. (Psalm 1:3)

Short Prayers to Start Your Day:

Lord I commit my day to you. As I realize you created this day, I willingly give my plans to you for this day. I speak Proverbs 16:3 over my day that says, "commit to the LORD whatever you do, and he will establish your plans." My commitment is to do what you intended for my life. I agree with Heaven and with my divine helpers today. Send my angels ahead of me to do your will on my behalf. Lord, direct me today, I give you full access to my plans and my day today

In Jesus name I pray,

Amen.

Lord, help me not to lean unto my own understanding but to rest in the fact that you have ordered each one of my steps for this day. I release my will for yours; I release my plans for this day for yours. Help me to release my control for you to be able take control! I am decreeing Proverbs 3:5-6 over my day. "Trust in the Lord with all your heart and lean not on your own understanding; in all your ways submit to him, and he will make your paths straight." What I do not understand, make it known to me that I may submit all my ways to you.

In Jesus name,

Amen.

Prayers for Warfare & Deliverance

Armor of God for Spiritual Warfare

"Put on all of God's armor so that you will be able to stand firm against all strategies of the devil. For we are not fighting against flesh-and-blood enemies, but against evil rulers and authorities of the unseen world, against mighty powers in this dark world, and against evil spirits in the heavenly places." *(Ephesians 6:11-12, NLT)*

Warfare Prayer

Heavenly Father, I come before You, recognizing the spiritual battle that surrounds me. I know that my struggle is not against flesh and blood, but against the spiritual forces of darkness. Lord, I put on Your full armor today—the belt of truth, the body armor of God's righteousness, the shield of faith, the helmet of salvation, and the sword of the Spirit, which is Your Word. Strengthen me to stand firm and resist the enemy's attacks. By Your power, I declare victory over every scheme of the enemy, for You have already won the battle.

In Jesus name,

Amen.

Deliverance from Spiritual Bondage

"The Spirit of the Lord is upon me, for he has anointed me to bring Good News to the poor. He has sent me to proclaim that captives will be released, that the blind will see, that the oppressed will be set free."
(Luke 4:18, NLT)

Deliverance Prayer

Lord Jesus, I thank You for the freedom You have given me through Your sacrifice. I acknowledge that the struggles I face are rooted in spiritual bondage. I ask for Your deliverance from anything that is holding me captive—whether it be fear, addiction, or any other stronghold. By the authority of Your name, I break every chain and renounce every lie of the enemy. I receive the freedom that You have promised, and I walk in the light of Your truth.
In Your mighty name,
Amen.

Overcoming Temptation with the Word of God

- "For the word of God is alive and powerful. It is sharper than the sharpest two-edged sword, cutting between soul and spirit, between joint and marrow. It exposes our innermost thoughts and desires." *(Hebrews 4:12, NLT)*

Temptation Prayer

Father, I thank You for the power of Your Word, which is alive and powerful. When temptation arises, I choose to stand on Your promises. Just as Jesus used scripture to overcome the enemy, I too will wield the sword of the Spirit. I declare that Your Word is my weapon, sharper than any two-edged sword, cutting through the lies and deceptions of the enemy. Strengthen me to stay rooted in Your truth, and let Your Word be my guide and defense in every trial.

In Jesus name,

Amen.

Prayers To Study In The Bible

- Psalm 51: A Prayer of Repentance
- Psalm 54: Answered Prayer for Deliverance from Adversaries
- Psalm 55: Trust in God Concerning the treachery of Friends
- Psalm 56: Prayer for Relief from Tormentors
- Psalms 57: Prayer for Safety from Enemies
- Psalms 60: Urgent Prayer for the Restored Favor of God
- Psalms 61: Assurance of Gods Eternal Protection
- Psalm 62: Calm Resolve to Wait for Salvation of God
- Psalm 63: Prayer of Fellowship with God
- Psalm 64: Prayer for Joy During Oppression

Biblical & Research Insights

Harvard Health. "Is Crying Good for You?" *Harvard Health Blog*, March 1, 2021. https://www.health.harvard.edu/blog/is-crying-good-for-you-2021030122020.

BibleStudyTools. "Declaration; Declare."
Orr, James, M.A., D.D., General Editor. "Entry for 'DECLARATION; DECLARE.'" *International Standard Bible Encyclopedia*. 1915. https://www.biblestudytools.com/dictionary/declaration-declare/.

Pew Research Center. "Religious Landscape Study: Demographic Information." https://www.pewresearch.org/religious-landscape-study/#demographic-information.

Sharefaith. "30 Powerful Scriptures on the Blood of Jesus." *Sharefaith Blog*, July 30, 2014. https://www.sharefaith.com/blog/2014/07/30-blood-of-jesus/.

YouVersion. *The Bible App*, Romans 6:6 (AMP). https://www.bible.com/1588/rom.6.6.amp.

YouVersion. *The Bible App*, Acts 12:1–19 (NLT). https://www.bible.com/bible/116/act.12.1-19.NLT.

YouVersion. *The Bible App*, Psalm 56:8 (NLT).
https://www.bible.com/bible/116/psa.56.8.NLT.

YouVersion. *The Bible App*, Psalm 120:1 (NLT).
https://www.bible.com/bible/116/psa.120.1.NLT.

Oxford Languages. "Posture." Google.
Accessed April 7, 2024.
https://www.google.com.

Additional Resources

Thank you for joining me on this journey of prayer and spiritual growth. Below are additional resources designed to encourage, equip, and strengthen your walk with God.

YouTube Encouragement & Teaching

Shae Speaks Truth
- Weekly encouragement, prayer, and biblical truth to help you grow in faith.
- ▶ youtube.com/@shaespeakstruth

Wee Move Ministries International
- Powerful teachings, prayer moments, and community ministry in action.
- ▶ youtube.com/@weemoveministriesint.6260

Join the Weekly Prayer Call
- We gather in prayer every week and would love for you to join us!
- Mondays & Wednesdays at 8:00 PM EST
- Dial-In Number: 425-436-6280 Access code: 758436#
- Let's seek God together in community.

Devotional Tools & Journals

- Find practical, faith-building resources at:
    - www.kcscribe.co

Available resources include:

- Invitation to Prayer Workbook – A guide to deepen your daily prayer life
- Rooted: A 90-Day Journal for Teen Girls – Build strong faith and identity
- Prayer Journal for Kids – Interactive and faith-filled for young hearts

Scan for more information and updates

GOD BLESS YOU!